SERIES

H. D. MYST

Copyright ©1999 by H.D. Myst.

All rights reserved.

No part of this book may be reproduced in any form or by any means without permission in writing from the publisher, except in the case of brief quotations embodied in critical articles or reviews. For information, please contact:

Simon & Northrop Publishing
3333 Midway Dr.
Dept. 102
San Diego, CA 92110

Manufactured in the United States of America
ISBN: 1-893181-20-0
Library of Congress Card Catalog Number: 99-63917

DEDICATION

I dedicate this novel to Janis, Patricia, Eleshia, Raktim, and Nilava. All who are from K.C.I. Also, Jen, Melissa, Cathy, and Andrew from L.C.I and Flora, Amy, Sue, and Nancy. I would also like to thank David B. I thank all of you for being so patient and supportive through out the whole production of this novel. Thank you.

"WHO'S THERE?"

Rebecca was getting sick and tired of this game of cat and mouse, so she headed back to the front of the salon. There was no one in sight. Rebecca turned around to see a message written on the wall. "Tanya, you always looked better with your natural hair color. Ain't that right...Rebecca?"

Rebecca began to back up from the wall. What she had just read frightened her beyond belief. Rebecca ran to the front door, only to be lucky to slip before the silent figure hiding behind the shadows of the door slashed a knife at her.

"So we meet again Tanya. I think it's about time you had a cut."

Rebecca looked up at the man. It was the same man from her visions. In his hand he clutched a sharp looking butcher knife. It gleamed like sinful evil. Rebecca tried to get up and run but her fall had somehow sprained her ankle. She was trapped...

PROLOGUE

When the past is unresolved...
When a past interferes with your present...
When a past threatens your future...
And above all, when a past hides a sinister secret...
You have Secrets of My Past.
The Past can kill...and it will!

March 2nd, 1947

The thunder crashed like a parade of beating drums in the silent night. Darkness covered the quiet streets of Peacefulville. A soft sobbing sound could be heard in the distance if you strained your ears. The sobbing was coming from an old Victorian house that looked like something from a painting. There was a marble stone pathway leading the way towards the front door. The inside of the house was breathtaking. There was a large spellbinding staircase, built to perfection. The oak wood of the staircase looked rich, as did all the exquisite furniture and paintings that surround the inside of this gorgeous house.

The staircase led to a large hallway full of mysterious bedrooms. Each bedroom held its own sinister secret. At the end of the hallway, there was a door with a beautiful design carved in the wood. Suddenly, the door swung open and a beautiful girl lay sobbing on her bed. Her bedroom was simply breath taking. There were cream colored silk curtains that were hand crafted. The queen size bed was to the far right. The sheets were made of a pastel violet silk.

To the left, was an oak dresser. The mirror that matched it was very enchanting. Close to the entrance to the room in the far right corner, was the girl's closet. It was filled with exquisite clothes - clothes that seemed to be made for a princess. Lightning flashed throughout the room. The girl was startled and looked up. Her green eyes were illuminated by the lightning which flashed through the room. Tears soaked her white silk dress, which hinted that she had just returned from a formal occasion.

The girl wiped her tears and stood up. The lights in the house were all out, due to the storm which caused a blackout on the entire street. The girl walked towards the beautifully decorated glass window. The girl's parents had specially made the window just for her. It was the only thing that she still had that she could remember them by, besides the silver locket that she always wore. The locket - she walked over to the full size mirror that stood directly across the room. The young girl looked at herself, and took the locket in her hands and held it tight. More tears came out of her green eyes.

As she held the locket in her hands, the young girl remembered the day she received the locket. It was such a happy time for her. It was her birthday. It was also the day she saw her parents for the last time. The girl read the inscription on the locket out loud.

"To our darling daughter, Tanya Annabella Arkenson. May you have all the happiness in the world. Always remember, we are always with you."

Tanya began to cry like she'd never cried before. But then, something strange happened. It was though a bolt of electricity went right through her body and she felt a shiver go down her spine. *Someone is coming. I can feel it. There is definitely someone in this house. Oh do not be ridiculous* thought Tanya to herself. *Honestly, my mind is so full of weird thoughts. What I need is to take a hot bath. That will soothe and relax me. All this stress will be taken away.*

"I better run a bath then, if I am ever to relax. I also better change into something a little bit more comfortable if I am ever to relieve this stress. I guess I'd better eat something as well. I am so famished. And, get some sleep. My beauty rest is required if I am to ever be fully beautiful."

Tanya got her bath ready and then proceeded to her closet. She had to choose a comfortable nightgown to wear so she could feel comfortable and get a full night's sleep. Tanya picked out a beautiful Persian gown which was a gift from her best friend Claudia Carmel. *Oh Claudia. I wonder where you are now. I wonder where all my friends are now.* Tanya lay the gown on her bed, and began to unlace her dress. The bodice was so tight, and made it so hard to breathe, that she thought she might faint.

"This stupid bodice. Why do these things have to be so tight? Honestly, I do not find these things lady like at all."

Before Tanya could finish changing clothes, the telephone rang. She smiled a little and quickly dressed herself again. After tying the laces on her dress, she walked over and picked up the phone.

"Hello."

Tanya waited for a response, but all she could hear was someone's constant breathing. "Hello! Is anyone there? May I ask who's speaking please?" Still all that she could hear was breathing. Tanya finally got frustrated and began to withdraw the phone from her ear. But then, suddenly, the mystery person began to speak.

"Don't put the phone down Tanya, or else."

Tanya shuddered. The voice sounded familiar - like a voice that she had not heard for many years. Tanya started to get that same strange feeling she had earlier. *Someone's here. Something is going to happen. Snap out of it. Put down the phone.*

"Look, I do not know who this is and I really do not wish to find out. Goodbye!"

"Don't you dare put down that phone Tanya!"

Tanya froze - *that anger, that fury. It couldn't be. It couldn't.*

Tanya was paralyzed in fear. The phone was still in her hand. "What do you want from me? Who is this?"

The voice was raspy. "I am coming for you my sweet and then we will live together forever. Just like Romeo and Juliet. Forever." Tanya began to cry again, but this time, with tears of fear. Tanya dropped the phone and began to pace across the room. Her eyes darted back and forth. *What should I do? What should I do?*

"The doors. I should lock all the doors and check all the windows."

Tanya ran downstairs. She locked the front door tight. The big bolts were for sure to lock anyone, or anything, out. There were similar bolts on all the windows in the house. Tanya checked the whole entire house to make sure that she bolted each and every window, and then went back to her room. On her bed, her diary lay open. The diary was wrapped in white lace and her initials were sewn onto the front cover.

Tanya went to the phone, and picked it up. There was no dial tone - the phone was dead. Suddenly, there was a loud bang. Tanya swung around to face the window, but there was nothing there. She went over to the window and realized that she had neglected to lock that one. Even though she was on the third floor of her house, she always made sure that there was no possible entry for a thief, or other such fiends.

Tanya fumbled with the latch and bolted the window shut. Then, the candles in her room began to flicker, casting shadows all over her walls. She had always found shadows fascinating - after her parents died, it seemed that shadows were the only things that were with her no matter where she went. They made her feel safe. But the shadows that were cast on her bedroom walls on this night were different from any kind of shadow she had ever seen. With her back to the door, Tanya took a deep breath and then tried to calm herself. *It's been a long day.*

Who could be doing this? Why me? I thought I was over all of this. I thought I was safe here. I guess I am not. I will never be free from the secrets that haunt me. A sudden creak made Tanya's skin crawl. She realized that the noise was coming from the staircase. *Oh no.* Tanya squinted her eyes. *Stop it. You are just over tired and hallucinating because of that stupid phone call.* Tanya's breath caught in her throat as, from the corner of her eye, she saw the shadow of an intruder.

As she built up her courage, she whipped herself around. Her long brown auburn hair flowed like an angel in fury. There before her, stood the man that she had dreaded - the man from the darkest parts of her childhood. "What are you doing here? How did you get in here?"

The man looked at Tanya and then began to snicker. "Do not be silly, Tanya. I told you that I would someday come back for you and reclaim the right that I have on you. I love you."

Tanya flinched at his words. "But I don't love you. I could never love you. I will never love you. You're a repulsive man. I am ashamed to even be associated with a scoundrel such as you. I suggest you leave."

The man's face grew tense, and then twisted in anger as he raised his fists. "If you wont be mine, you won't be anyone's. I will have you. You will always be mine."

The man walked menacingly towards Tanya. Before she could even scream, his strong hands pushed her into the direction of the window with an immense force that slammed Tanya against the window. As pieces of glass scattered on to the floor, Tanya's locket slipped off of her neck and fell into the vent below her feet. Glass stabbed into her face and body as her screams echoed throughout the silent streets of Peacefulville.

Tanya started to descend towards the ground. Her thoughts were filled with confusion. *Why me? Why did he do this to me? Help me!*

I don't want to die; I don't want to... Tanya's thoughts could not be finished, for she had hit the ground snapping her neck in half, and twisting her arm violently. As she lay on the ground, rain soaked her once beautiful white silk dress which became swirled with different shades of red, from her blood. Tanya was dead.

The figure of the man loomed from above, as he watched her from the window. His thoughts were full of devastation, but also joy. He finally had his revenge on her. Now even in death she could not belong to anyone else. He knew that she would be waiting for him when he died.

"Like I told you. If you will not be mine, you shall not be anyone's."

The man then left the scene, not noticing that her silver locket had dropped on to the vent. The locket slowly started to slip and then it finally fell into the vent, but it did not go far. It got tangled up. What a tragic death. Tanya's body lay on the grass like a squirrel that had just been run over. She never had a chance to say good-bye to her family, friends and especially the love of her life.

October 16th, 1984

Deep within the hallways of the dorm slept a young girl. The girl had been having trouble sleeping for a number of nights, and on this night, she twisted and turned in her bed, slamming her hands against her mattress. Strange echoes and sobs were heard emanating from her room. She was having another nightmare - another nightmare of her.

Her. It was a person who she had never seen or met before in her life, but, strangely, she felt as if she had known this other girl her entire life.

"Rebecca, wake up!"

Voices pulsed through the silky blanket that had covered

Rebecca's face. She felt safe and also warm. She didn't feel like waking up at all. She was still trying to make out the strange dream that she just had. It was a dream like she never had before, and she could remember everything that happened in it:

Let me tell you about the events that led to my death. I remember falling through darkness. At first I thought it was a dream, but then I understood that I had fallen. My hair flowed like an angry fire, and my dress was torn in shreds. I finally hit the ground. My body felt wet, and I could not move or speak. I heard thunder and lightning in the distance, and there, beside me, I saw my blood swirling in a puddle of water. But, surely enough, it did not bother me. I felt calm, peaceful and at ease.

That's when I realized that I wasn't breathing anymore.

"Rebecca wake up! Wake up or else you are going to be late for work."

The voices continued to pulse through the security of the blanket. Rebecca felt peaceful even though she was having another nightmare - but only this time it wasn't a nightmare. This time, to her, it was something even more. A tear streaked down her soft, ivory skin. Rebecca flinched a little remembering the dream that had followed that one.

In my dream I can remember myself wearing a beautiful gown of some sort. It was white with elegant ruffles on the sleeves. Also I remember that an old newspaper called the Capital Star was laying open and left by someone on an antique garden table. The page was A12, and there was an article about a girl.

"The body of an 18 year old girl was discovered this morning by local police. The girl was found contorted on the ground, amongst pieces of broken glass. Police believe that it was just another teen suicide. The girl's identity has not be released as of yet."

Rebecca felt sympathy for this girl who was unknown to her.

There was a picture of the girl next to the article, so Rebecca picked up the newspaper to look at it. She could not breathe. It was a picture of her. Rebecca tried to scream but nothing came out - she was paralyzed in fear. - *It can't be. I am still alive. I am not dead. Not dead, not dead.*

"Wake up! Rebecca you idiot! Wake up!"

Rebecca's eyes slowly opened, allowing the light of the room to be seen. She opened her eyes and then shut them again for a minute, reopening them slowly. She had totally lost track of the time. She had to get ready, or else her boss was going to have a major shit fit again. Rebecca had been arriving late for work for the past week, due to her lack of sound sleep. Her boss said that was no excuse.

Rebecca had that in mind when she bolted out of her bed. She hurriedly gathered her clothes and ran to the bathroom to take a quick shower and let the hot water soak all over her body. It was so relaxing. After her shower she got dressed and went back to her room where she saw Cathy and Julie, her best friends.

"Look, I know that I am late again and I am sorry."

Julie made a face as well as Cathy. "You were having another bad dream weren't you, Rebecca?" She tried to avoid the question. "Hurry up you guys or else we are really going to be late." Julie grabbed Rebecca's arm and sat her down on the bed. "Cathy and I are not going anywhere until you tell us the truth. Were you having another nightmare?"

Rebecca nodded her head. Julie and Cathy knew about Rebecca's nightmares from the beginning, and they knew that they started soon after her parent's sudden death. Rebecca began to shed tears of sadness thinking about her parents. She remembered how she had to stay at the hospital when her parents were in that car accident. She remember the whole event as if it were yesterday.

Rebecca was excited about her seventeenth birthday, and her parents decided to throw her a special birthday party. Rebecca had no clue what they had planned for her. As usual, Rebecca went to school and walked back home. She noticed that the door was unlocked and that there was no sound coming from inside the house.

"That's odd. Where could everyone have gone? May be they forgot that today was my birthday."

Rebecca grew sad. She walked into the house, but she did so cautiously, because the door was already open. She tried to turn on the lights but they would not turn on. Rebecca walked into the hall, which was like a living room. Suddenly, she heard a marvelous sound.

"Happy Birthday Rebecca!"

Rebecca's eyes grew wide with tears of joy and happiness. *Wow, they didn't forget me.* Julie ran up beside her holding a large gift. "This is from your parents. They went to go get your cake, but they'll be back soon."

Rebecca took the gift from Julie's hands and started to unwrap it. "Wow, it's that book that I have been wanting to read! Julie, thank you for giving it to me on my parents behalf."

Rebecca was too overwhelmed. She finally got the book that she had been dying to read for many months. The book was called, "The Enchanted Being." Rebecca gave Julie a big hug, as everyone gave Rebecca more gifts to open.

Things were going perfectly, when suddenly...

There was a knock at the door. Rebecca ran to the door and opened it and saw two police officers standing in her doorway, with their hats in their hands. "Are you Rebecca Bailey?" Rebecca's stomach began to knot. "Yes. I am. Why?"

The police officer lowered his eyes. "Miss. Bailey, I am sorry to say that your parents were killed in a severe car accident this afternoon. I am so sorry."

"No. No. NOOOOOOOOOOOO!"

Rebecca started to cry hysterically, then suddenly stopped and fell down, crashing her head onto the hard marble floor. "Becky!" Julie ran over to Rebecca's side.

Rebecca looked up towards Julie and the police officers. Everything began to drift from her mind - everything. Rebecca snapped out of her memory when the sound of the hair dryer interrupted her. She looked to see Cathy blow-drying her hair.

"Well this time I think your nightmare was worse than before. You were not acting yourself, Becky."

Rebecca looked at Cathy. "What do you mean by that Cathy?" Cathy nodded her head. "Becky you were speaking like another person. I couldn't make out what you were saying, but trust me. Your voice sounded like it was coming from the other side of the grave. Come on, let's go you guys. We do not want to be late."

Cathy and Julie left the room while Rebecca got her keys and then followed. She turned around one last time and mumbled. "The other side of the grave.... I wonder."

CHAPTER 1

The leaves were scattered everywhere. Autumn had finally arrived. To Rebecca autumn was a very beautiful season. She enjoyed watching all the leaves fall. The colors were so beautiful, though it did tend to get a little bit too chilly during this time of year. She walked silently down the street, on her way to visit a sick friend.

"I wonder if Kristen is feeling better?"

Kristen was one of Rebecca's good friends. They had known one another for about three years. Cathy and Julie did not like Kristen, but for Rebecca's sake they tried their best to get along with her. They said that Kristen was a phony that only used people for her own means and gains. Rebecca knew that this was not true at all, because she knew Kristen like no one else did.

Kristen was a very pretty young girl, but Rebecca's friends agreed that out of all of them, Rebecca was definitely the prettiest. She had long blond hair that reached to her elbows, green eyes and smooth ivory skin - almost like a piece of silk. Rebecca had the most beautiful smile. Her smile could enlighten a dark and dreary day. Everyone liked Rebecca around, and there wasn't a day that they'd wish to be without her company.

But Rebecca was always putting herself down. She did not like it when people said nice things about her, and she could not understand why everyone thought she was pretty. She found nothing pretty about herself. Her attitude towards life was great, and she was very ambitious, with many hopes and dreams, but something inside her made her feel that none of them would come true.

Rebecca finally made it to Kristen's enormous apartment building. Rebecca loved to go over to her friends' houses, but in Kristen's case, she avoided it because she was terribly afraid of heights. It was a fear that she had ever since she was a child. She would not even go to her bedroom window, for fear that she would fall out.

Worst of all, Kristen lived on the top floor of the building - level twenty - the highest level of the building. Rebecca flinched at the thought of how high Kristen lived, as she walked up the stone steps towards the front doors. Once inside, she searched for Kristen's buzzer number.

"Let me see now. Umm, there it is. Kristen Kemp. Number 220."

Rebecca punched in the numbers and waited for a response. "Hello?"

"Hello Krissy, it's me Becky. Let me in."

"Oh, okay."

Rebecca heard the buzz and hurriedly unlocked the front door. Rebecca walked into the main hallway of the building. The building gave Rebecca the creeps, and it smelled of decay. She could tell that the building was quite old because the paint on the walls had begun to chip. The carpet was dirty and the elevators were always out of service.

Rebecca walked over to the stairs but there was a sign on the door saying that they were not to be used. "Great. Now I have to use the elevator. I hope I don't get stuck in it like last time." Rebecca pressed the button and patiently waited for the elevator to arrive. There was a little ringing sound indicating that the elevator had arrived. The doors slowly opened and Rebecca walked in and pressed the button. The door shut and the elevator moved smoothly with out hesitation. *Please don't get stuck. Please.* "Ding."

Rebecca was so relieved that the elevator did not get stuck this time. She let out her breath and walked down the dark hallway to Kristen's door. Rebecca waited a minute before knocking on the door.

I hope Keith is not here. If he is I will not hear the end of it. Many different voices could be heard behind the locked door. Rebecca strained her ears, trying to hear to whom the voices belonged. The door opened, and there, standing in the front door of Kristen's place, was Jeremy, Cathy's boyfriend.

"Yo yo yo, wuz up?" Rebecca made a funny face at Jeremy. *Where does Cathy find such unusual boyfriends? Gosh, he is so warped. Utterly weird.* "Hi Jeremy." Rebecca shoved Jeremy aside and walked into the apartment. "Kristen, where are you?"

"I'm in the bedroom. Give me a minute."

Okay thought Rebecca. *Please come out soon cause I don't really feel like putting up with Jeremy's non-important, not to mention stupid, conversations.* Rebecca walked into the living room. She was surprised to see Cathy, Julie, Lana, and David there as well.

"Hey guys! What are you all doing here?"

David and the others looked up and saw Rebecca. "Hey Becky, long time no see, Babe. What's new and exciting?" Rebecca smiled. *That silly David, he always was a charmer to women.* Rebecca had a secret crush on David ever since grade school. He was one of her favorite friends in the whole entire world, and he knew everything about her - everything.

"I am great, now that you're here." Rebecca gave David a big bear hug. "I missed you so much. How are you?"

David smiled and then looked at Cathy and the others and frowned. "Not so great." Rebecca noticed the serious looks everyone had on their faces and then she started to get worried. "What happened? Why are you guys acting so serious?"

Cathy smiled. "Well Becky, that's just it! We were just acting. Great ain't it?"

Rebecca made a face. *What the hell is she talking about?* Rebecca could not make sense of what Cathy had just said, so David made it clear. "Becky, we were acting to see how'd you react. We all joined the drama club. We are going to be in the play this year. Guess what?" Rebecca looked at David. *Oh no. No. No. No. He didn't do what I think he did.* "You didn't do what I think you did... did you?"

David nodded his head. "We signed you up as well. This years play is called, *Midnight Twilight*. Great title isn't it?"

Rebecca did not respond. When David looked at her, he could tell that she was not very pleased. Rebecca did not like to do anything fun-involving being in front of many people that she did not know. But Rebecca was not about to argue with David or the rest of them today because she did not have the strength to do so. *Maybe I will have a good time. Acting will probably make me forget about the nightmares that I have been having.*

"Look, I'm sorry if you're upset. But you have got to stop hiding from people. I mean, ever since your parents died, you have totally shut out your friends. It isn't fair and I am not going to just sit around and watch you throw your life away. No way."

David was expecting Rebecca to get mad and yell at him but instead she ran up to him and hugged him, with tears running down her cheeks. She was not used to getting yelled at by anyone. Only her parents yelled at her when she had done something wrong, and now David did. *My parents used to yell at me because they cared about me. David cares a great deal about me and I really don't want to disappoint him, or any of my friends, for that matter.*

"Thank you David. I am sure I'll have fun acting. I mean we will all have fun acting together."

David took Rebecca away from his arms and looked at her. *Boy, she is a hot number indeed.* David also had a huge crush on her ever since grade school, but he did not know how to tell her. Cathy got up from her seat.

"Well if this dramatic moment is over, I suggest we all get ready to leave." Rebecca looked at Cathy in confusion. "Where are we all going?"

"We have a drama class today. So, we have to go to the school auditorium and set up the stage." Rebecca nodded her head. *Great. This is going to be fun.*

The auditorium was cold because no one had used it for many months. When the lights were turned on, Rebecca got a better view of the auditorium. She was a bit surprised because it was the first time she had ever been there, even though she had been going to this college for about two years. Rebecca loved college. She shared a room with Cathy and Julie, and it was fun living in the dorm with all the other students.

Of course the guys were not allowed to be on the girls floor at all, but at night they came down anyway to visit their girlfriends and friends. *Gosh I wish someone would come and visit me. Not that I need a man in my life right now. He would probably think that I am crazy for not trying to sleep. I hate to sleep. I know that if I sleep I'll have dreams of that girl. - of Tanya.*

Tanya was the name of the girl that Rebecca had been having strange dreams about. She did not understand why, but she honestly wished that she knew.

Rebecca remembered how nervous she was when she received the letter saying that she had been accepted by Heartland College. She had always wanted to go to there, and now she could. Good ol' Heartland College. It was such a great college. *I feel so good when I am here. I feel like I have been here at Heartland all my life. But that is really a silly thought.*

"Okay, listen up gang. We all have to clean up the auditorium and set up the props. So let's do it."

Such motivation! Well that's Julie for you. Rebecca watched as Julie instructed everyone on what they should do. She was born to be a leader. That was one of her best qualities.

Julie had long brown hair and she had a lot of freckles. She was tall and very skinny. She wasn't beautiful, but she was a very beautiful person on the inside and that illuminated her on the outside.

On the subject of beauty, there was also Cathy. Rebecca thought that she was as beautiful as a princess, and always reminded her of royalty. Cathy had a slender body and excellent shape - her thighs were picture perfect. She was a size one - very petite and very wanted by every guy in school. Her hair was natural. It looked like she had it curled everyday, but that was natural as well. Cathy's attitude was also very royal. But the one thing that Rebecca envied was that Cathy knew how to do everything without help from anyone. Cathy was a very independent young woman, and for that, Rebecca thought that Cathy was the most beautiful of all the girls.

David had a different kind of beauty - sexy. To Rebecca, David was the ultimate definition of sexy. He was the most outrageously good-looking man that she had ever seen before in her life, with short black hair and a great buff body. His mischievous smile made Rebecca think that she was in heaven. His sensual and charming voice just blew her over. But one thing stopped her from admitting how she felt about him - David was her best friend.

Rebecca thought if she admitted how she felt and things did not work out between them, then their friendship would also be destroyed. She could not let that happen under any circumstances. She cared too much about their friendship and she would never do anything to destroy the bond that they had.

Rebecca finally stopped gazing at David and walked to the back of the stage, looking for garbage and other things they could use for their props for the play. A dark shadow watched Rebecca form the corner of his eyes. She stood up and suddenly felt a cold chill crawl down her spine. *What is that strange feeling? I feel that there are eyes watching me but I do not know where they are coming from. I am beyond silly. I am totally safe here. It's all because of those stupid nightmares that I have been having - those stupid dreams.*

Rebecca was standing right under two large sandbags, and she continued to feel like she was being watched. Suddenly, a strange image formed in her mind. She could see David running towards someone yelling for them to watch out. Rebecca shook her head. *Jeez, you watch to many romance movies.* Rebecca laughed to herself and continued to search for things.

The dark shadow was now near the ropes which released the stage curtains and the stage props. He took his hand and released one of the ropes. "Lights, camera...action."

Rebecca heard a loud thump, and she turned around like a whip. "What was that?"

Rebecca heard another thump, and this time, the others heard it as well. "What the hell was that sound? Becky, you okay?"

"I'm fine. What is that?" David nodded his head.

Lana came running back in with news for everyone. Apparently, someone had broken into the science lab and taken four jars of termites. *Who would have stolen jars of termites?* It was weird.

Rebecca shook her head and walked around to see if she could find some props. Everyone set up the stage and started to rehearse their lines. They all rehearsed for a couple of hours and then called it quits. Rebecca and the others started to clean up the stage.

Rebecca heard a strange sound. She strained her ears and then she heard something that sounded like footsteps. She followed the noise until she came right into a dead end. Rebecca looked around, but there was nothing but dirty clothes, a trunk and some old textbooks. Rebecca was getting scared and her muscles became very tense. She could feel in her veins that something was about to happen.

The dark and mysterious man that watched Rebecca from the shadows untied another rope, this time releasing the sandbags that were directly above Rebecca. They began to fall with great force. Rebecca looked up just in time to see the bags coming right for her.

"Help me!"

But before the bags could land on their target someone came to her rescue. "Watch out." Rebecca turned her head slightly to see David grab her just in time. Both jumped out of the way before the bags hit. Rebecca looked to the side and saw four empty bottles that looked like jars from the science lab.

The bags finally landed and crashed right through the stage. Rebecca slammed herself against the floor and so did David. They both heard a strange sound, as though the stage was about to collapse.

Rebecca looked at David in total fright. "David the floor! The floor is going to break!"

"Guys, get off the stage!" Julie and the others ignored what David said and walked over to them both. But before they could reach them, the remaining sandbags fell and crashed through the floor beside Rebecca. Before she could escape, the entire floor gave away and she fell through it. Cathy and the others stopped in their tracks. David quickly got up to his feet and ran to see if Rebecca was all right.

All David could see was darkness - pure darkness. "Becky, Becky, are you alright? Rebecca. Answer me! Don't worry, I'm coming to get you. Hang in there." Suddenly, Cathy had a strange feeling and looked up, only to catch a glimpse of a shadow disappear. *What was that?*

Meanwhile, Rebecca was unconscious. She had hit her head against the floor before it collapsed. She was swept away from reality and into another one of her nightmares. She was in a dark room that smelled of hot wax and incense. Rebecca felt as if she had been in this room long ago but could not remember when and where, or why. *Why?* Rebecca asked herself this question. *Why am I here? Why do I keep having these nightmares?* No matter what Rebecca did, she could not wake up. Her body felt weak and heavy. There was a strange smell in the air like...like gas. Rebecca had been knocked out by gas, not by the bump on her head, even though her head was hit very hard.

Please help me! Somebody help me! Rebecca struggled to open her eyes but couldn't. But she did not give up, and finally she was able to regain consciousness. Her vision was blurry, and all she could make out was a shadow of a figure. There was someone else there besides her. She tried to move, to call for help, but she couldn't. *David, oh David where are you?*

David was held back by Cathy and the others. He had scraped his head and there was blood all over the stage. Cathy turned David around to face her. "David, you're hurt. You can't go down there. Jeremy and I will go and find Rebecca." David tried to get away, but the others held him back. Jeremy and Cathy climbed down the hole in the floor.

"Jeremy, what's that smell?" He started to sniff the air. "Holy shit! It's gas. Oh my god, Cathy stay here. Make sure you get the others out of here." She made a face. "But...but...?" Jeremy looked at Cathy. "Don't worry, I'll will be okay." Tears were forming in her eyes, but she smiled and then quickly gathered the others and left.

Jeremy held a flashlight because it was so dark underneath the stage. *I hope Becky's all right.* Jeremy examined the drop. *Boy, that was sure a big drop. I didn't even know the drop was that steep.* Rebecca thought that she was hallucinating because she could have sworn that there was someone else with her, but now she couldn't see anyone.

She got up slowly and coughed from all the dust. "What the hell is this place? I didn't even know that there was a place like this. I have to find out how to get out of here." Rebecca walked right into Jeremy. Both got startled. "Oh Becky, thank God I found you. Are you okay? We have to get out of here fast cause there's a gas leak. Let's go."

Jeremy had Becky in his arms as the two made their way out of the auditorium. Once outside, the others rushed over to Rebecca. "Rebecca, are you okay?" Rebecca, who was still in a daze because of the gas and the bump on the head managed to shake her head, and then she started to remember something. *That shadow. Maybe I should tell them that I thought there was someone else down there with me.*

Rebecca coughed a little. "Guys, while I was down there I could have sworn that there was someone else down there with me." David raised his eyes and so did Cathy. Cathy hesitated but then remembered what she had thought she had seen. "When the floor broke, I thought I saw a shadow of a person run away, but before I could get a better look they were gone. Maybe someone was there."

David, who was concerned with Rebecca's well being, agreed with Cathy that maybe there was someone else there and maybe, just maybe the person who was there was responsible for the sand bags falling. As for the floor breaking, that might have been also pre-planned as well. But then the question is, who would do that? And why?

"You guys, that's impossible. I think that the bags fell by accident. I mean no one has used the auditorium for months. Maybe the last people who used the auditorium didn't tie the ropes in a proper knot or something. Also, the termites. Maybe the termites were released near the drama room and decided to have a munch on the stage. Maybe that's why the stage collapsed. About Rebecca seeing someone, it could have been that she saw Jeremy. I mean he did go down there to get her. Maybe we should think things through logically before making any strange assumptions. Don't you guys agree?"

Julie made a very good point. Even Rebecca believed her. *But I could have sworn I saw someone else down there besides Jeremy. But maybe it was Jeremy. I couldn't see very well, anyway. But the floor. The floor broke. It broke like a piece of paper. I don't know what to think.*

Lana came running towards everyone with Mr. Peters, Mr.

Lindale and Mr. Hiller. Mr. Lindale came up to Julie and asked if she was all right. Rebecca thought, *wait a minute, I'm the one who fell through a hole and he goes to ask Julie if she's all right. Well, that's because Mr. Lindale was a twenty one year old student teacher from Kingston university and boy was he a babe. A sight for sore eyes. At least I have David. My David.*

Mr. Hiller hurriedly got everyone one out of the building and called the ambulance, concerned that others were in danger by the gas leak.

David limped over to Rebecca and gave her a warm hug. "I'm glad you're all right." Rebecca smiled. "Thank you for trying to save me. But as usual, you're always late. I mean I could have died down there." David smiled at what Rebecca had just said. They always teased each other whenever something serious happened. It was the only way to make the situation seem less tragic.

Mr. Hiller approached Rebecca and David and asked if both were okay. Then he turned around to ask what had happened. After Cathy finished explaining about the sand bags and the floor falling, all of them were then taken to Clement Valley Hospital for a brief check-up to make sure if they didn't inhale too much gas.

At the hospital, everyone got a clean bill of health except Rebecca. She had hit her head quite hard. Also, David had a deep cut on his forehead, but otherwise both were healthy. Rebecca told the Doctor about her constant dizziness and her terrible nightmares. She also explained her fear of sleeping because she didn't want to have any more bad dreams and nightmares.

The doctor told her that she should see a psychiatrist and stop worrying so much. She also inquired about volunteer work at the hospital, deciding that it was the best time to ask since she was already there. She had always meant to become a volunteer, but she had never gotten around to signing up. *Maybe this is what I need. I can do some work and help somebody. Maybe I can also sleep better without hav-*

ing any more nightmares.

Rebecca would be starting her volunteer work in two days, and she was excited. She was dropped off at the dorm by Cathy and Julie, who decided to go to Kristen's house and try to get the day's frightful events out of their systems. Rebecca wanted to do that too, so she changed her clothes and lay on her hard mattress, closed her eyes and tried to retrieve the dream she was dreaming when she was knocked out. But it was hard for her to go to sleep. It was only five-o'clock and she usually didn't go to sleep until about ten. But she gave it a try anyway.

The dream seemed like more than just a dream to her - it seemed more like a memory. Rebecca concentrated some more. Finally, she was back in the dark room with the hot wax smell, but there was also another smell. She sniffed it and decided that it smelled like decay of some sort. She walked around her dark room to the end where there was a mirror. She hesitated a little then approached the mirror.

Her muscles were tense - she was scared. Rebecca blinked her eyes, and then a scream rose from her throat. The reflection was of the dead girl Tanya Annabella Arkenson! Rebecca froze in fright. *Why? Why is she here again? Where's my reflection?* Rebecca started to cry, not noticing two bony hands reach out from the mirror. Rebecca lifted her head, but was too late.

The hands grabbed her and drug her into the mirror. Rebecca screamed until she finally was let go by the hand, and she fell to the floor. Her eyes were closed in silent pleading to whatever it was that pulled her into the mirror. All she wanted was to be left alone. She couldn't hear anything, so she opened her eyes slowly and looked all around the new room that she was in.

It was exquisite. There were antique lamps and beautiful satin curtains covering the gigantic windows. Rebecca stood up and looked around the room, trying to see if the thing that had pulled her into the room was still there with her, but she couldn't see anything.

She was relieved. But then, she saw another mirror in the room.

"I don't know if I want to look in it or not."

Rebecca took a deep breath and walked towards the mirror. She was relieved when she saw her own reflection, but there was something different about her. She noticed that she looked much healthier and well proportioned. She was better looking then ever and her hair was curled to perfection. She was dressed in a beautiful gown. She felt so enchanted in it - like a princess.

A princess. What a feeling. I feel like that I have felt this way before, but when? Rebecca did not care at the moment, she felt so happy. She was startled to hear a man's voice calling her from across the room, but when she turned to look, she saw a handsome young man with a gorgeous smile and an expensive suit. His hair was slicked back and he looked wonderful. *Wow, maybe I am finally having a good dream. He's probably my prince and I must be his princess.*

"You look like a vision darling. I could eat you like a piece of delicate chocolate." *Wow, I've never been compared to chocolate before. This guy is awfully sweet. May be I should comment on how he looks.* "Well, the same goes to you my good man. My night in shining armor. Will you dance the night away with me? I would be honored to be in your arms."

The mans lips formed a smile. A killer smile. "But of course. I wouldn't have it any other way. Come let us go to the ballroom. The guests will be waiting for us." Rebecca smiled, and let the gentleman escort her down the extravagant stairs, with rich red carpeting. The ballroom was overcrowded with people who were dressed up in fantastic attire. The room was decorated with balloons and ribbons.

Rebecca thought she had died and had gone to heaven. It looked like a fantasyland from a storybook. She felt that she was on top of the world and that all her stress and worries could never reach her. A nice looking couple approached Rebecca.

"I am so glad that you could make it. It took you long enough. Now go on up and give your speech."

Rebecca was confused. "A speech you say? For what may I ask?"

The girl who had spoken to Rebecca made a shocked face and then replied to Rebecca's question. "You were chosen. Therefore, you must go on to the podium and give your speech."

Rebecca smiled. *I must have won a pageant, or something. This is so fantastic.* Rebecca was escorted to the top of the podium by the gentleman with her, which she thought was funny because she had no idea who he was. *But he is so cute*, thought Rebecca. She stood in front of the room in everyone's view. A funny looking man handed her a microphone.

She coughed and then proceeded. "Good evening my fellow friends. I am honored to be here today at this enchanting gala event. This place has never looked so beautiful and all of you have never looked so marvelous, as well." The people started to applaude. Rebecca smiled. But before she could go on, a young woman came walking on to the podium with another microphone. The woman's face was covered with a mask, but Rebecca could tell that she was beautiful.

"We are glad to have you here as our special guest of honor. Do you mind if I ask you some personal questions before we go on with the gala?"

Rebecca smiled and shook her head. "All right then, first question is who is the man you love and what is his name?"

Rebecca turned a little red and then started to answer. "Well, that is a very easy question and the answer is..." Rebecca noticed that her date wandered onto the stage. He placed his arm around her and then came up to her face and gave her a kiss on the cheek. *Who does this man think he is? What is he doing?* "What do you think you are doing? I do not love you, I love Jack."

Jack. Who's Jack, thought Rebecca. *Why did I just say Jack?* "Pardon me. What I meant to say is that I love David. He is my best friend and also the man of my dreams. I will always love David. Always. No one else could ever take his place in my heart."

Rebecca's date gave her an evil sinister stare. *Did I say something wrong? I mean I just gave my honest answer.* The guy snatched Rebecca's microphone from her hand and lightly pushed her. Rebecca was flabbergasted. *How dare the stupid brute snatch my microphone and push me.*

The man then raised his fists and knocked Rebecca down to the floor. As she fell, the floor beneath her broke and she crashed through the hole - just like the hole at the auditorium. She landed in Tanya's bedroom. It was very familiar, for she had seen this dream many, many times. Plus, it was the place where the murder took place. The murder that haunted Rebecca's dreams every night.

What am I doing here? Rebecca looked to the side to notice a calendar on the wall. "March 2nd, 1947." She was shocked. *This is 1947. What am I doing here? For heaven sake, I wasn't even born yet.* Rebecca slipped on a piece of paper that was on the floor and bumped her elbow against the bedpost. As she lay there, she noticed the time - 8:55pm. Rebecca stood up like a soldier. *Oh my God. It can't be. I am in the nightmare that I always have. Then, where is Tanya? Why is she not here?*

She walked all around the room only to catch her reflection in the large antique mirror. There in front of her stood an image of Tanya instead of Rebecca. *What? It can't be.* The door to the room opened, and a familiar looking figure walked into the room. Rebecca's eyes grew in fear. *No. No, it can't be.* The man found Rebecca and then threw her into the wall beside the window. Rebecca remembered. *The window. He's going to throw me out the window! I don't want to die again! I don't want to die again!* But before Rebecca could run, the man grabbed her by her shoulders and then said his last words.

"Goodbye Tanya. If I can't have you then no one else can. Not even David. Sorry Becky." A scream rose from Rebecca's throat. But it was too late. He had thrown her out of the window. The glass shattered and Rebecca fell through the window, but she managed to grab the ledge. The glass crashed onto the ground making a screeching sound. The man was displeased that Rebecca did not fall. Rebecca was holding on for her life, but her blood made the ledge very slippery. Blood dripped down her arms.

Rebecca looked up at the man's face, but it was covered. He was wearing a black trench coat. She looked into his eyes, pleading for her life, but the man did not care. He pulled out a large knife that gleamed like a sinister monster that only wanted to taste blood on its blade - her blood.

"If you won't die the easy way then you are going to die the hard way, bitch."

The man slashed his knife at Rebecca's hands and she tried to dodge his blade. She started to worry. *I can't keep dodging his knife forever. I have to let go.* Rebecca remembered what she had learned in her high school gymnastic classes - concentrate and believe. These two elements can get you through anything. But only if you put your mind to it. Rebecca let go of the ledge just in time to avoid having her wrists cut. She landed on her feet.

She did not take the time to look back and see if the man was behind her. She just kept running as fast as she could. Then, a strange noise suddenly woke her up.

"Ah."

Cathy and Julie were startled that Rebecca woke up so suddenly. Rebecca was sweating and her pulse raced very fast. Her head throbbed. She could feel the blood pumping through her veins. *What a horrible dream!* But this time she was able to run away from her nightmare, something she could never do before. It felt good to run away with out looking back.

"Sorry to wake you Rebecca. We tried to be as quiet as possible." She was relieved that Julie and Cathy had woken her up. *I don't think I could have lasted long in that dream. I mean that nightmare.* "No problem. I think I slept a little bit too long anyway. What time is it, by the way?"

Cathy looked at her watch. "It's about 2:30 am. Sorry we came in so late."

Rebecca was surprised. *I can't believe they spent practically all day at Kristen's. I mean since they don't like her that much. I am so shocked that I slept that long. I don't feel tired any more. I don't think that I'll be able to sleep but may be if I try...*

"Did you guys have fun at Kristen's?"

Julie smiled. "Yes, I guess we did. Enough talk. I am bushed. Sorry Rebecca. Goodnight Cathy! Goodnight Bec! See you all in the morning. Oops! See you in a couple of hours. Good Morning everyone!"

"Goodnight Julie! Goodnight Bec! I mean Good Morning!"

"Good morning everyone! Sweet dreams."

Rebecca yawned and the turned off the lights. *Good morning and good night again.* Rebecca kept her eyes opened as long as she could. Cathy and Julie were already fast asleep when a cold draft came into the room. It felt like a sign of infinite evil. A man with a black overcoat watched the girls sleep as he took out a long, sharp knife. He spoke quietly.

"Soon, very soon."

Then he disappeared. Rebecca turned in her bed in discomfort and opened her eyes. *I can't sleep.* She got up and put on her robe. *I think I will take a short walk in the hall.* Rebecca crept out of her room and strode up and down the hallway. Finally, she was exhausted and able to return to bed. She was calm and was now looking forward to her first day as a volunteer at the hospital. "Maybe then my troubles will go away."

It was Monday and the evening was wonderful. Rebecca was happy and relieved not to have had a nightmare for the past two days, and actually get some sleep. The sleep would do her good, since she had to go to the hospital for her volunteer work.

Rebecca walked into the hospital wearing tight stone washed jeans and a tight blue matching body suit. She avoided the elevator and took the stairs to the fifth level, where she was supposed to get her clothes and instructions. She had a bad feeling about the elevator.

She changed into her uniform and then proceeded with her assigned duties. She found that helping others made her feel happier with herself, and she enjoyed helping others feel and get better. When she had finally helped her last patient, she went to the cafeteria for her break. She was very hungry, but didn't eat anything thinking that the food in the cafeteria could get anyone sick from the looks of it.

So Rebecca just bought a coke and headed back to her floor where she was surprised to see Julie, Jeremy and Lana. She was also relieved that Jeremy had brought some take out from the Doghouse, the restaurant where they had all first met. Cathy was a waitress there and had spilled some Pepsi on Rebecca, but she did not get mad. She told Cathy that it could happen to anyone. After that, Rebecca and Cathy and the others all started hanging out there and became very good friends.

"What are you guys doing here? Please tell me that the food is for me."

Jeremy smiled. "Well, we all thought you might like a Doghouse special instead of the cafeteria food, so we bought it for you. Here, eat it and then hurry up and let's go."

"Go where?"

Rebecca took the takeout bag from Jeremy's hands and then started to attack the food inside, stuffing her face with French fries. "Your shift is over in about three minutes and we have to go to the police station and tell them what happened at the auditorium at school."

Rebecca nodded. Julie, Lana and Jeremy went to the elevators, and Jeremy pressed the button. When the elevator arrived, everyone got in except Rebecca. "Rebecca, get in here already." She shook her head. "No. I don't have a good feeling about this. I'll take the stairs. You guys go. I'll meet you." Jeremy made a face and then grabbed Rebecca's arm and pulled her in as the doors to the elevators closed.

Rebecca crawled into the corner of the elevator. She had a bad feeling about this. *Stupid Jeremy.* The elevator was taking forever. The radio announced the news.

"Doppler radar shows that a major thunder storm is currently over Peacefulville. There is a storm advisory in effect, and all citizens should stay indoors as much as possible."

Suddenly, Rebecca had a feeling that a bad incident was about to happen. Then the elevator stopped with a jerk, causing them all to fall down. "What's going on? What happened?" Lana heard the news. "There was a blackout. That means we are stuck in here."

This is what Rebecca was afraid of. The elevator began to jerk some more. Jeremy kicked at the door and shouted for help. Lana boosted Rebecca, so she could push open the trap door that was on the top of the elevator shaft. Rebecca looked all around and saw that the elevator was stuck between two floors. She strained her eyes to see the top of the elevator shaft, but saw nothing. There was only total darkness.

Lana cried out. "Rebecca, do you see anything cause you ain't that light, you know." Rebecca made a face and replied, "The elevator is stuck between two floors and it's pitch dark. I can't see anything. Wait, do you smell that?"

Everyone in the elevator stuck their noses in the air and took a sniff. Jeremy's face twisted in fear. "Holy crap, it smells like something's burning. Oh shit! The wire that's what's burning. Look!" Everyone looked into the direction that Jeremy was pointing. The elevator wires were burning. Lana couldn't hold on to Rebecca anymore so she dropped her and she landed on top of Jeremy.

Lana looked at Rebecca apologetically. "I am so sorry Rebecca. You may look light but your not. Are you okay?" Rebecca was mad, but there was no time for that. "I'm fine, no thanks to you." She looked at Jeremy. "Sorry Jerry, didn't mean to land on you." Jeremy smiled. "No problem Becky."

While the group was planning a way to get out before the wires burned, a dark shadow of a man watched them all. In his hand he carried a long sharp knife that seemed as if it was his companion. Everywhere he went he had his trustworthy knife. Soon, very soon, he would get rid of that troublesome girl, Rebecca Bailey. In order to continue living as a free man, he must get rid of that problem standing in his way.

With his face twisted in anger, he raised his knife and began to cut the first wire of the elevator, making it jerk violently. Rebecca noticed that the elevator was tilting to its side. "You guys something is happening." Everyone stopped and felt the elevator shake and move.   Meanwhile, in the lobby Cathy, Kristen and David waited in the dark for the others to arrive. It had been a while and they all agreed that something must have happened to them. David started to get worried. He felt that Rebecca was somehow in trouble. Cathy started to get worried as well, and Kristen was frightened by the news of the storm.

"I wonder if they're okay." Kristen looked at David and Cathy. "Look guys, I am sure that they will all come falling to our feet before we know it. Great, the lights are back on."

David felt better, and he hugged both of the girls.

The Shadow Man continued to slash the elevator wires until there was only one left. *Oh, this is going to be a dramatic ending. I will wait for the right moment.* The Shadow Man held his knife, while he watched the trapped teenagers fight over of how to get out of the elevator. He found this very amusing.

Tears poured out of Rebecca's eyes. *I am going to die. I didn't even get to tell David that I love him. Oh God, please.* Jeremy thought of his girlfriend Catherine. He remembered how they first met. It was summer and Cathy had a summer job at the beach as a lifeguard. Jeremy had seen her around and decided he liked her, so, to get her attention, he had pretended that he was drowning. Cathy ran over and helped him. He gave her a kiss and she pushed him into a sandcastle, telling him that he was an idiot.

Jeremy was not about to give up that easily, so he pursued Cathy until one day he found her all alone sitting in the rain. She had been crying. Her date had tried to put the moves on her and she fought him off. The guy called her a cheap whore and then made her get out of his car. When Cathy saw Jeremy, instead of getting mad she ran up to him and gave him a hug.

Jeremy took her to his apartment so she could dry off, and he made two cups of hot chocolate. Cathy told him everything as she sat on the couch with Jeremy. She was happy that she decided to get to know him. She felt better after she talked to him, and then their lips met and they shared a romantic embrace. After that, they started dating and had been together for almost three years. *Oh Cathy. I love you.*

Lana was not thinking of anyone special, she was just scared to death. Julie, however, was thinking about Mr. Jonathan Lindale. She knew that he had liked her in the past and probably still did, but she was too uncomfortable with him being a student teacher. She did like him, but she was not sure if it was appropriate to date an older man. She was seventeen and Jonathan was in his twenties, but he was a babe. But then again, so were all the teachers at the college.

Everyone was holding onto the bars in the elevator, trying not to move the elevator and cause it to fall down the shaft. The elevator screeched as it tottered. When the Shadow Man positioned his knife, the blade gave off a reflection that shone in Rebecca's eyes and she looked up. "What's that light?" But before she could see the Shadow Man, the elevator started to fall.

"Hang on!"

The elevator fell like a heavy brick. It started to gain speed as it started to fall farther down the elevator shaft. Rebecca, regardless of the fact that the elevator was falling stood up. The force of the fall made her knees wobble, but she continued to stand as straight as possible. After a few seconds she became dizzy and fell, smashing her head against the railing. Jeremy caught her as she landed.

Rebecca was swept into another dream - another nightmare. This time she was in a cemetery, wearing Tanya's white silk dress. The dress was soaked in blood. *Is the blood hers, or is the blood mine. What am I doing here?* Rebecca turned herself around and saw a sign with the name of the cemetery.

"Clevont Cemetery."

I think I've heard about this cemetery before, but that's impossible. If I'm in Tanya's time, then that means that this cemetery exists which means that maybe Tanya exists. No. No. It can't be! Rebecca began to walk around, but then she stopped in her tracks. About ten feet across from where she stood stood the man who stalked her in her dreams, looking even more sinfully evil then before. The Shadow Man raised a weapon. Rebecca was shocked at what the man held in his hand.

The Shadow Man now held a razor sharp machete. Rebecca started to hyperventilate. *Oh god, help me. Maybe if I talked to him.*

"Please don't hurt me. I haven't done anything wrong. Leave me alone."

The man didn't care. He raised his machete and proceeded towards her. With each stride, he came closer and closer. Rebecca screamed and ran for her life. *I need to get as far away from him as I can.*

Rebecca ran behind a tombstone, breathing irradically. She wiped the sweat off her forehead as her eyes scanned the name on the tombstone.

"Oh my God. To our Darling friend Tanya Annabella Arkenson. You will always be with us in mind, body and spirit."

The sound of a footstep made Rebecca jump. The Shadow Man had found her. He slashed the machete at her, missing her face by an inch but managing to cut her shoulder. Blood poured out of her wound. The pain stung. Rebecca got up and ran as fast as her feet could carry her. She ran out of the cemetery and stopped in front of an old familiar-looking house.

"That's Tanya's house. Well, I guess it's better then waiting to be chopped to bits."

Rebecca ran inside the house and locked the door, waiting silently.

Jeremy had his arms around Julie, Lana and Rebecca as the elevator continued to drop. He knew that the collision between the elevator and the floor was going to be intense. The basement of the hospital consisted of boarded up floors that were not in use. When the elevator crashed, it would go right through the main floor and then through the unused floors, until it finally reached the bottom.

David, Cathy and Kristen were informed that their friends were trapped in the crashing elevator. Cathy started to cry, while David prayed that the impact of the crash would not be too hard - it was all they could do.

Rebecca waited in silence - the Shadow Man hadn't come. Maybe she lost him back in the cemetery. She got up slowly and flinched in pain. She had been cut very deep, and her shoulder was still bleeding. She got up and searched for a first aid kit, or something that she could wrap her shoulder with. She also needed to find a weapon in case the Shadow Man appeared again.

"What a bloody bastard that man is. Attacking an unarmed

woman in such a way. So uncivilized, I say."

Rebecca roamed the dark halls of the house. The sky was getting dark as dusk arrived. She found a kitchen that was every chef's dream and much more. There were two refrigerators and every type of kitchen appliance ever invented. The oak table was painted a dark burgundy color, and the shelves were the color of the dark midnight sky.

Rebecca felt strange in this kitchen. *Why do I feel like I am at home?* Rebecca shook off her feeling and searched the drawers for something that she could wrap her shoulder with. When she finally found a piece of cloth, she wrapped her shoulder up tight and grabbed a metal stirring stick - *just in case.*

Rebecca was scared to leave the safety of the house, so she decided to explore it. She crept out of the kitchen and into the living room. She was stunned by what she saw. The living room was like a sanctuary, with photos of Tanya all over the place. *She was a very beautiful young woman* thought Rebecca. She looked at all the pictures, but one in particular caught her eye. It was a picture of Tanya and her friends.

Tanya shared the picture with three boys and three girls. One of the boys was holding Tanya as if he were her boyfriend. Rebecca felt as if she knew these people. *Impossible, they are probably old and wrinkly.* Rebecca pulled out the picture from the frame and was surprised to see a signature by everybody who was in the photo.

"Group picture of Amy Winchester, Samantha Peters, Steven Lancaster, Daniel Peters, Claudia Carmel and Jack Skye. Wait, Jack!"

Rebecca remembered that she had said his name when she was answering a question in her previous nightmare. *Jack. That must be Tanya's lover. Then why did I say his name?* Rebecca heard a noise and turned her head around. She saw nothing. She heard some movement coming from the chimney and suddenly, Santa Claus appeared.

"Oh my god, this has to be a dream cause I stopped believing in you when I was four. I am never eating a Doghouse special again."

The Santa Claus chuckled jollyly, then walked over to Rebecca and handed her a gift. "For me. Thank you but don't think that I believe that you are really Santa Claus." She opened the gift to find the card. *Okay this is weird.*

"To: Tanya Annabella Arkenson, May all your Christmas wishes come true. From: Santa Claus."

Rebecca threw down the card and started to yell at Santa. "Look you, I am not Tanya. You are the man who knows everything, don't you know who I am?"

Santa Claus looked at her. "Oh, I know who you are Tanya, the question is do you know who you are?" *What is this man talking about?* She was so frustrated that she let down her guard for a second. When she raised her head Santa had disappeared.

"Santa, where are you? Where did you go?"

Rebecca walked carefully around the living room, clutching the stirring stick in her hand. She spotted a hairpin on the ground and bent over to pick it up. Behind Rebecca, Santa Claus stood. An evil smile spread across his face, as he changed out of his costume - the Shadow Man now stood behind Rebecca with his machete. He was ready to strike but before he could, she saw his shadow and quickly turned around, slamming the metal rod at his face and knocking him down to the floor. She snatched the machete from his hand and ran up the spellbinding staircase.

Rebecca had almost reached the top of the stairs, but the Shadow Man was there first. In his hand he held Tanya's locket. "You want answers, find this and you will get your answers. Looks can deceive you and so can your… balance." And with that he pushed her. *What's with him and pushing me?* Rebecca fell backwards and tumbled down the stairs.

When she opened her eyes, she was looking at Jeremy. Finally she came back to reality. *Oh my god, the elevator. We are falling. Oh no*. The elevator zoomed and zoomed. It reached the ground floor with a great bang. The floorboards underneath broke with force and the elevator continued to fall.

It crashed through the last floor with such an impact that the elevator door broke and the four were tossed out like rag dolls. There was the smell of something burning in the air - the floor that they had crashed into started to catch on fire. Rebecca landed on a piece of wooded board. The pipes in the elevator shaft burst and a stream of gas leaked into the burning room. It was as hot as a volcano that had just erupted.

Jeremy, Julie and Lana had landed on a desk of some sort. Either way, they were trapped with no way out. A stream of gas surrounded Rebecca. Jeremy yelled and shouted for her to wake up but she was unconscious, once again. Rebecca was doomed. The Shadow Man smiled. *Finally that witch will be desecrated properly.*

"May you burn in peace...Tanya."

CHAPTER 2

The fire continued to spread its unmerciful flames with rage, hate and revenge on its mind. It was as if it was saying, who dared awaken me from my sleep? I shall destroy everything in my path for doing such a thing. The fire spread quickly over the floor like water. Now the room that Jeremy, Lana, Julie and Rebecca were trapped in looked like a burning inferno of death.

Jeremy shouted to Rebecca who lay unconscious on top of the wooden platform. The gas streamed over her and surrounded her. *It's barbecue time* thought The Shadow Man, as he watched the action take place. He would have stayed to view his long lost archenemy pay her final dues, but he heard a noise from the elevator shaft in which he was hidden.

"We have got to get out of here. But we can't leave without Rebecca."

Jeremy didn't know what to do. All he could think about was losing Cathy and one of his best friends to whom he never told that he cared and appreciated her friendship. He couldn't let Rebecca die. No way. He promised Cathy that he would look after Rebecca as if she was his little sister.

Lana and Julie continued to scream for help, as the fire drew closer. Lana's eyes searched the room for a way out but the brightness and the heat of the fire stung her eyes. Julie tried as well, but couldn't help but close her eyes. Lana ducked her head as low as she could. It was then that she saw a door.

"Jeremy, I found the door. Come on let's get Rebecca and get out of here."

Jeremy nodded his head. *I have to get to Rebecca, and fast.* Jeremy found a blanket and wrapped it around him before he jumped off the table, landing close to the wooden board. Jeremy took the blanket and blocked off the fire that kept him for reaching out for Rebecca. She was scooped up into Jeremy's arms and then, along with Lana and Julie, was carried out the door.

The door led into the underground tunnels. "Shit, we must be at the lowest level of the hospital. This door leads to the town's sewer. Come on."

Jeremy and the others hurried as fast as they could. As Lana ran, she turned around and saw that a stream of gasoline was trailing closely behind them with a blazing fire that looked like an angry train just waiting to run over whatever was in its path.

"Guys, run. The fire is gaining on us."

The Shadow Man was not pleased. *Damn. That witch got away again.* The Shadow Man disappeared.

Meanwhile, David, Cathy and Kristen got news that Rebecca, and the others got out of the room and now were somewhere underneath the town. David and the others left the hospital, so they could save their friends.

Julie ran for her life, and Lana followed. Jeremy was a little behind the two because he held Rebecca in his arms. She had started to come to. "My head. Oh my god. Where? What? The elevator. Oh my god we crashed. What's?"

Jeremy told Rebecca not to worry. She was groggy and confused when she turned her head to see the fire gaining on them quickly. She began to panic. Her stomach twisted. *Oh no. Please. Not another dream. I don't want to see anymore nightmares. No more!*

David, Cathy, and Kristen had finally got to the manhole that was close to the hospital. "If the they are down there, they will probably come down this way." Cathy made a face. "How do you know?" David smiled. "Trust me. I have taken my ex girlfriend down there. Let's just say I know my way around town." David opened up the manhole and climbed down the ladder. He could smell gas and also he could feel the flames.

Jeremy saw light at the end of the tunnel. He kept on running. Finally, the three reached the end of the tunnel and found David. "Thank God man. Take her. Everyone get up now." No one hesitated at all. Everyone climbed up the stairs just as the wave of fire passed by them.

Cheers could be heard by the crowd outside waiting and watching David's rescue. Rebecca smiled in relief but then fell into a dream. Her body went limp in David's arms.

"Rebecca. Rebecca. Speak to me Rebecca. Rebecca."

A tall, handsome police officer finally made it on the scene, and saw Rebecca's limp body and ran over to David. "Let me see. Her pulse is very weak. Put her on the ground."

David did as the police officer said. As David stared in horror, Rebecca suddenly stopped breathing. *No! She can't die!* The officer then started to perform mouth to mouth on Rebecca. He put his hands on her chest and began to push.

Rebecca could still feel the heat surrounding her, but it was not the same type of heat as before. No, this time the heat was more within then out. Rebecca found herself in a small, but cozy looking living room. She was sitting on the couch with a very handsome man. He looked like a movie star, with his well defined features and slicked back hair. *He kind of reminds me of David.*

She noticed that she was wearing Tanya's white silk dress. *I hope this isn't a nightmare.* The handsome man inched closer to her, and then, out of nowhere, he grabbed her hand and began to rub it. Normally, Rebecca would have felt invaded, but on this occasion she felt nothing but warm sensations running through her body. She felt her hormones go into a rage - a rage she hadn't felt in a long time - a rage that she had only felt when she used to be with Keith. But now, she felt this rage with this man.

"Tanya, you are so beautiful. Do you know that? Of course you do."

The handsome man then placed his lips onto Rebecca's soft sensuous lips and their mouths collided with intense hunger and passion - a feeling of fire. Rebecca was aware of what was going on but did nothing to stop it. She felt as if what she was doing with this man was right somehow.

"I love you Jack. Please, show me how much you love me. I am yours forever."

Jack then started to unlace Rebecca's dress, revealing her bare shoulder. His lips quivered as they landed on it, and a chill of sensation crawled down Rebecca's back. Rebecca's curious hands undid the buttons on his shirt revealing his gorgeous body. She gazed at his muscular features, thinking that he was very handsome. *What a man.*

She was in pure ecstasy, with no cares in the world. But why did she feel so comfortable doing this with someone she didn't even know? She did not know why, but there was something so very strange about this whole thing. Rebecca felt as if she had done this before, with the same man.

Jack removed the dress completely and Rebecca's body was in full view. He trembled from all the sensations that ran through his body as he stared at the woman that he loved and would always love. Jack finished taking off the rest of his clothing, when suddenly Rebecca began to fade and disappear. Then she suddenly reappeared.

"What the hell is going on here?" Jack ignored what she said and continued to kiss her. Rebecca became frightened, not understanding what was happening to her. She was also having trouble functioning clearly, due to her hormonal rage. All she wanted to do was to jump on top of Jack and ravage him until he begged for mercy.

Rebecca now lay on the couch. Jack passionately inched his way on top of her body, caressing her everywhere and anywhere. Rebecca moaned in pleasure. *I feel so good. I feel as if this is right. But why? I should stop him. But a part of me wants him. I can't decide what I want.*

Jack kissed Rebecca like a savage. He began to move on top of her. She didn't know what to do. All she could do was lie back and enjoy this feeling of freedom. The feeling of passion. The feeling of fire.

"Is she breathing yet?"

David stood by the officer who was performing CPR on Rebecca, who nodded his head and continued on. Meanwhile, Rebecca lay in Jack's arms. The passion that they shared was incredible. She could not believe what had just happened to her. She knew that this must have been a dream, but what a dream it was. She had never felt so fulfilled in her life. She was in complete ecstacy. Jack slept silently, as Rebecca watched.

"My handsome fella. I want to be with you, my love. If anything were to happen to me I would want you to move on with your life. That's how much I love you."

Rebecca reached up to Jack's face and planted a romantic kiss on his forehead, and slowly got up to put her dress back on. She noticed that there was a balcony and she decided to get some fresh air and enjoy the beautiful scenery. From where she was, she could see most of the town, but it looked completely different.

There were old buildings and houses and stores that looked old fashioned. *Well that's because I am in Tanya's time*, Rebecca told herself this as she continued to admire the scenery. A screeching sound made her stand up straight. *What was that?* Rebecca listened a little bit more and then walked back into the apartment and saw that Jack was missing from the couch.

"Where could he have gone?"

Rebecca heard the shower. *He must be taking a shower.* A smile turned up on her face. *May be I should join him then.* Rebecca pranced like a ballerina into the master bedroom to find Jack's clothing scattered on the bed. She crept into the bathroom. There was a lot of steam so she couldn't see Jack clearly.

Rebecca smiled. She opened the door so that some of the mist could leave the bathroom. *Jack and I will make our own mist.* She unbuttoned her dress and placed it on the stand, and wrapped herself in a towel, waiting for the right time to enter the shower and surprise Jack.

Rebecca turned to face the shower and noticed that there was something written on the fogged up glass:

Rebecca I know who you really are, but do you know who you are? Maybe I have to tell you... My way.

She heard a scrapping sound which made her turn around in frenzy. *Oh my God he found me again. Where is he? Oh my God, where is he. I know he's here. Where's Jack? Maybe he got him. I need a weapon.* Rebecca searched the bathroom and found nothing but a pair of scissors. She held the scissors as if her life depended on it, and looked outside the bathroom door. Nothing in sight. She backed away from the door.

Rebecca turned around to see a new message on the fogged up glass:

If you want know where I am, all you have to do is repeat 'Shadow Man' three times and I will appear. Then we can talk about this whole thing as civilized adults. What do you say?

I am not sure about this. But maybe he will leave me alone. "Okay, alright. Shadow Man, Shadow Man, Shadow Man."

Nothing happened. There was no sign of anyone. *That loser tricked me.* "Okay, I did what you told me to, where the hell are you?" A dark, horrid voice spoke. "Look closely, I am right before your eyes."

What? Rebecca looked at the shower screen, slowly opened it and screamed. She thought that he would be behind the screen but there was no one. *Thank God. He is just playing a sick joke. He gets his jollies by making me scared. But I am not going to be scared.* Rebecca closed the door and started to laugh out loud. But then she stopped. She turned back around to face the screen door.

"Crash."

Oh my god. Suddenly, the Shadow Man appeared through the glass screen door, with a large, blood covered kitchen knife in his hand. "You better run as fast as you can, 'cause I am going to get you this time and there is no way you are getting out of here alive."

Rebecca turned around and began to run. The Shadow Man was not far behind. She suddenly slipped and fell to the ground, and turned to see the Shadow Man facing her. Although she could not see his face, she could tell that it was twisted with bittersweet hate towards her. His hand quivered with the knife. He raised it high and then, without warning, plunged it at Rebecca. She moved quickly and jabbed the scissors in the Shadow Man's leg, causing him to fall to the ground.

However, he still managed to cut Rebecca's arm, and blood began to pour out of the wound, dripping everywhere. The Shadow Man howled in pain. Rebecca ran to the door only to find that it was jammed. The only way out was the balcony and she was on the eighteenth floor. She ran out to the balcony and stood on the railing. *I have no choice. He can't hurt me if I don't want him to. This is my dream and I am in control.* The Shadow Man appeared on the balcony and slashed the knife at Rebecca's ankle. She slipped off the railing and fell.

"Stand back. All clear."

The officer used an electric charge on Rebecca. David and the others waited silently and prayed. Then, she twitched her eyes and started to wake up. Rebecca was falling and falling, but before she hit the ground, she suddenly disappeared. Rebecca opened her eyes. Her vision was blurry for a brief second but soon it became clear. Her eyes focused in on the handsome officer that was in front of her view.

"What happened? Who are you?"

The officer turned around and smiled at David. "She's going to be okay."

He then turned to Rebecca. "My name is Inspector Carmicheal. Adam is my name. Nice of you to join us back into the living. Here's my card if you want to get in touch. It's not everyday I meet a really attractive young female."

Rebecca almost choked. The officer was hitting on her. *Cool.* That had never happened to her before. David ran to Rebecca and gave her a hug. He didn't want to let go of her, so the others cried and joined in. The Shadow Man watched them from a distance.

"She's okay. Damn. Looks like I am going to have to find her weakness." The Shadow Man noticed David and the others. "And from the looks of it, I think I may have already found out what it is. Say bye bye to your friends Rebecca."

The Shadow Man left thinking over his next step into eliminating Rebecca once and for all. Rebecca thanked Adam for reviving her. All she wanted to do was go home, but David wanted to spend time with her and he couldn't do that if she went back to the dormitory, so he took her to his place for the night.

Rebecca walked into David's apartment and admired it, as she strolled into the living room and sat down on the couch. She looked at David as he locked the door and went to the kitchen to get a hot cup of Cocoa for her. She smiled, realizing that she really did love David a whole lot. She took a few deep, relaxing breaths. *Wow, what a week. Falling sandbags attack me, I fall through the auditorium stage, I get into an elevator that falls down and I was caught in the middle of a fire and I...*

Rebecca's thoughts shifted to Jack. *I also did it with Tanya's man. I should feel ashamed of myself but I don't. Even though it was a dream, I can't help but feel like it wasn't. It felt real. Almost too real.*

David returned with two hot cups of cocoa. "Here you go Becky," he said as he handed Rebecca the glass. She slowly blew into the cup before she sipped it. The sensation of chocolate was exhilarating. *Chocolate. I love chocolate but I know it's not very good for me. It could also make me fat.* A sudden fear of getting fat made Rebecca put down her glass of cocoa.

"What's wrong? Why aren't you drinking your cocoa?"

"I just don't feel like drinking it, that's all."

David made a surprised face and continued to drink his. He inched his face closer to her's. She could feel his breath a few inches away from her neck. *So close but so far away.* Rebecca knew that even though he was so close as a friend, she couldn't tell him that she loved him, because then their friendship might be lost.

David suddenly backed off. *What the hell am I doing? Rebecca will think I am an idiot if I tell her that I like her. This could completely ruin the friendship we have and I don't want that to happen.* David got up. "Becky, I am going to sleep. You'll be all right?"

Rebecca paused but then responded. "Sure. Go to sleep. Goodnight."

David left the living room. Before he went to bed he shouted goodnight to her. Rebecca had tears in her eyes. *Maybe it is about time that I stop dreaming of being with him cause it isn't going to happen. Maybe I should move on and find another fantastic guy.* Rebecca got up to put her cup away, when a card fell out of her pocket.

It was the card Adam had given her when she awoke from her last dream. *Adam. Maybe I should give him a call. I mean, he did seem awfully friendly and he did show me that he was interested in me. Dating a police officer. Mom would be proud.*

She put the card down and pulled out the sofa bed. She lay in the bed and covered herself with her nice fuzzy blanket, and went to sleep. Cathy and Julie finally arrived home. It was not exactly home since the two lived with Rebecca in a dorm room, but it was close enough for them to call it home. Since Rebecca was staying at David's house, Kristen decided to stay over the night.

"So guys, what are we going to do? Our classes start on Wednesday and it's only Monday."

Cathy changed her clothes while answering the question. "Well, I have to have to go to the recording studio and record my music video for my project. You guys are welcome to join me."

Julie made a face because she suddenly remembered that she had to go to the library, which was off campus. "I have to go to the library on Maple Berry, but Kristen can go with you."

Kristen nodded her head. Julie got her keys to her car and left. Cathy got her stuff and left. Kristen said that she wanted to take a shower, change her clothes and then she would meet Cathy there. She finished her shower and put on her green dress. Then she locked the door to the room and left.

***

"We are going to get in shit if the Dean catches us."

"Shut up you moron."

Alec and Mike crept silently in the hallway of the girl's dorm. Alec was going to meet his girlfriend Stacy and he was going to introduce Mike to her friend Laura. But Mike looked a little scared. For some reason, he always got paranoid whenever he was with Alec.

"Look man, I have to go the washroom. Wait for me."

"But, but..."

Alec looked disappointed, but then he left to go the bathroom. Mike waited patiently, but he heard a noise that scared him. He decided that he should go back to his room, so he turned and left Alec in the washroom.

***

Kristen stopped in the middle of the hallway. She thought she could hear footsteps following her from behind, and she turned back. "Hello, is anyone there? Hello." Kristen shook her head and started walking faster, but the faster she walked the faster the footsteps behind her sounded. She started to run. She ran down the hallway and into the stairwell. She ran up the stairs and snuck behind the corner and waited to see if there was actually someone following her.

Nothing. She began to sweat and her heart pounded. *I got scared for nothing. All this paranoia is going to give me a headache.* Kristen laughed out loud and then turned around. A dark looming figure stood in front of her. In his hand he had a sharp axe with a shining blade. She screamed and tried to get by the man, but he slashed the axe at her.

Kristen moved out of the way of the axe, but she was in such shock that she didn't notice the two strong hands come at her with such a force that she fell down the stairs. She smashed against the cold floor, cutting her. Blood began to pour out of the wound. The Shadow Man slowly walked down the stairs. Kristen struggled to get up, and when she finally did, she ran into the hallway in the direction of the recording studio.

Rebecca slept peacefully in her bed, but suddenly Rebecca started to feel pain in her stomach. She opened her eyes and got out of bed with sweat dripping down her head. *What a strange feeling.* She put some clothes on. *I don't know what this feeling is but something inside me is telling me to go back to school. I feel like someone is in trouble.*

David heard a noise outside in the living room, and when he got up to investigate, he saw Rebecca putting on her shoes. "Rebecca, where the hell do you think you are going? It is one-thirty a.m."

"I know it is. I am going back to school. I fee like someone is in trouble. I know that sounds crazy but I feel like someone I care about is in trouble. I'm going with or without you."

David made a tired face. "Give me three minutes and I will come with you."

Rebecca was happy. Not at the fact that David was going to come with her, but that she could finally answer Cathy's question, wondering what David wore to sleep. *The answer is boxers. I am in heaven.* David came back out and then they both left.

Kristen ran down the hall, her blood leaving a trail behind her. Tears streamed down her cheeks. *I have got to get to Cathy.* She finally made it to the studio, opened the door, and ran in.

***

Alec unzipped his pants and then went to the bathroom. After he was done, he zipped his pants back up and went to the sink to wash his hands and fix his face. "I am going to get lucky tonight." He took out his cologne and sprayed himself with it. A noise in the bathroom made him turn around. "Mike is that you? I told you to wait outside for me."

No answer. "Look you little shit, I am not in the mood to play around, so get the hell out from wherever you are, or else I am going to have to beat the living crap out of you. Do you understand me?"

Alec heard the door open and then close. *What a loser* thought Alec. *Mike got scared and left the bathroom.* "That's how you take care of morons." He smiled at him self. He thought he was the biggest stud in the whole school. He got himself ready to leave but he didn't get very far because behind him stood the Shadow Man. Alec was pissed now.

"Oh I am so scared. Can't you see me shaking in my booties?

What a loser, Mike."

Alec laughed. The Shadow Man raised his hand in which he held an axe. Alec stopped laughing. The Shadow Man lunged his axe at him, but Alec caught it and smashed his arm into the Shadow Man's face. The Shadow Man grabbed Alec's neck, and with one hand raised him into the air. Alec tried to get himself free but he couldn't move.

The Shadow Man spoke, his voice full of amusement and hatred. "You really want to know how to take care of morons? Like this."

The Shadow Man threw Alec into the mirror. The glass cut Alec and he fell to the ground. The Shadow Man grabbed him and flung him into a toilet stall. "Let's see how long you can hold your breath under water," he said as he pushed Alec's face into the toilet while Alec struggled to get free. He tried to kick the Shadow Man but he struck Alec's leg with the axe. Alec fell to the floor - his air had started to run out.

The water started to invade his lungs, and all Alec could feel was the suffocation. He couldn't breath. The water finally made it's way into his mouth, and Alec was no more. His body went limp. *One down, two more to go.* The Shadow Man picked up Alec's dead body and left to find Kristen.

***

Kristen was trembling in fear. Never had someone tried to kill her before. She didn't know which room to go to because there were too many rooms and Cathy could be in any one of them. Kristen heard a scrapping noise. *Oh no.* She yanked the door shut and then opened a door and ran inside.

She looked around Recording Studio One. The lights were turned off and the place was a mess. Kristen kept her eyes glued to the front door, and she nearly tripped over the wires that were on the floor. Her eyes caught a glimpse of Cathy in Recording Studio Two, which was right behind the one she was in. All that separated them was a soundproof glass window. Kristen saw Cathy sitting on the chair with earphones on, so she ran to the window and started to bang on it, hoping that Cathy would see her. But she had no such luck. Cathy was listening to her music video. Kristen stopped banging on the window, feeling the icy cold breath of the Shadow Man on her neck. She turned around and a scream came out of her mouth. The Shadow Man grabbed Kristen by the neck and threw her into the sound proof window.

Cathy did not hear a thing. She just kept on listening to her music video, wondering what was taking Kristen so long. Rebecca and David finally arrived. Rebecca went running into her room to see Julie at the computer typing away. "Rebecca, what are you doing here. I thought you were staying at David's?"

"I was but I have this feeling... that someone is in trouble. Where are Cathy and Kristen?"

Kristen grabbed the camera stand that lay next to her on the floor and whacked the Shadow Man as she started to run. She dashed out of the room and into the hallway once more andran upstairs in to the direction of the janitor's office. Unfortunately, she was stopped by a hand which grabbed her and threw her against the wall. The Shadow Man was angry. He walked up to Kristen and picked her up. "Say your prayers."

Rebecca, Julie and David walked into the recording studio and spotted Cathy. Rebecca asked where Kristen was and Cathy told them that she was supposed to meet her but never showed up. *I wonder where she is? I guess she is having the time of her life at some party somewhere.* Kristen constantly left without telling anyone and she always ended up at some rave, or party and she would come back the next day.

Rebecca looked around the studio and saw that Studio One had blood on the window. "There's blood on the window. Oh my God. Kristen. Kristen must be in trouble." Before the others could absorb what Rebecca had spotted, or had said, she ran out of the studio in search of her friend.

The Shadow Man threw Kristen through the second story window. He had no mercy for anyone. It was nothing personal against Kristen, or the other innocent people, but he had to have his revenge on Rebecca - Rebecca his beloved. The girl who betrayed him. The girl who, even in death, could not be his. But now he would get his revenge. He was going to make sure that he took away everyone that Rebecca was close to. He was going to make her suffer.

Kristen's helpless body slammed on to the cold ground covered with dew. A chilly breeze blew across her lifeless body. Her neck snapped and her arm broke when she fell. She died on impact. The Shadow Man smiled and then left to find his last victim of the day.

***

Mike walked down the hallway, scared and worried because Alec had not shown up, and it had been over an hour. He decided to go back to look for him. When he opened the bathroom door, he was exposed to the broken shards of mirror scattered on the floor. *What the hell happened here? Where's Alec?* A noise in the bathroom startled him, and he turned around to see a large knife gleaming at him.

The Shadow Man emerged from one of the stalls and walked slowly towards Mike. It was an easy kill - Mike was paralyzed with fear. The Shadow Man raised his knife and got in his killing position.

***

Rebecca searched up and down the halls for Kristen but could not find her. *This campus is so big, she could be anywhere.* Rebecca sighed but then noticed blood on the ground, and followed it to the front entrance of the boys' washroom. Rebecca placed her hand on the doorknob and began to twist.

The Shadow Man plunged the knife down into Mike's chest. A yell came out of his mouth and he fell to the floor in an instant. Rebecca heard the scream and ran inside. There she saw Mike bleeding to death on the floor. She ran to his side and tried to comfort him.

"Are you okay? Who did this to you?"

Mike couldn't speak. All he could do was stare. The Shadow Man appeared behind Rebecca, holding his trustworthy knife. He raised it up and got himself ready to strike. He wanted to make sure that he had the pleasure of killing Rebecca. He wasn't going to kill her as quickly as he had the others. He wanted to see her suffer.

Mike tried to warn Rebecca, but she was tending to his wounds. David and the others heard her cries and went running in her direction. Mike was dead. Rebecca slowly got up and walked out of the boys' washroom. Tears soaked her dress. The Shadow Man followed her, still holding the knife.

David turned the corner just before the Shadow Man struck Rebecca. He escaped before David or the others could see him. "Rebecca are you okay? We heard your cries."

Rebecca explained what happened and Julie called the police. Adam arrived on the scene. He held Rebecca in his arms, comforting her. David gave them both a vile and angered look. A short time after Kristen's body was discovered. Rebecca and the others began to cry, grieving for their friend.

Adam told Rebecca that Kristen was thrown out of the second story window and her neck was broken as well as her arm. Her death was just like Tanya's. Rebecca's head started to hurt, and she started to sway. Her vision started to blur and her body began to ache. She had a flash of Tanya's death, showing a man pushing her out of the window, and then it was gone. She then had another flash and she saw the Shadow Man holding Kristen in his hands. Rebecca was shocked. *It can't be. This can't be what happened. The Shadow Man threw Kristen. Kristen's body crashed through the window and then fell to the ground.*

Rebecca almost choked. *What is going on? Why am I seeing such horrifying things? My cruel mind is playing tricks again. I can't take it. I hate who ever killed my friend. I hate him.*

The next day, Rebecca went to the police station to answer some questions about the murders. They thought she would know something, since David thought he saw a man about to strike her with a knife. Rebecca had no information at all. All she knew was that her friend was dead. She was such a good friend to her, and she could never imagine that someone would want to hurt Kristen, or herself.

Rebecca, Julie, Cathy and David were dismissed from school for a week to grieve for the loss of their friend. A week later Rebecca finally called up Adam and arranged a date with him. She needed to get all the pain off her mind and she didn't want to bother David, or the others. The date wasn't as she thought it would be.

Adam took her out to the ball game and then they went dancing, which did not seem very romantic to her. Things were going great until the two had a disagreement on something and then they both ended up in a huge argument. But David had seen the two of them share and embrace at the restaurant, and he was pissed.

Rebecca couldn't help it any longer. She wanted to tell David how she really felt about him. She wanted to know what he felt for her. She had promised Kristen that she and David would go out together and be more then just friends and she was going to honor her promise. It was Kristen's wish for them to be together. She had told Rebecca that she thought they both belonged with each other.

The rain poured down, and Rebecca walked outside David's building waiting for him to come home. She had already waited for an hour, but she was going to talk to him no matter what. David came about three minutes later. He parked his car and walked to the front door. When he saw Rebecca he said hi, and then continued to walk inside.

"David. I want to talk to you and this time I am not letting you go until I finish talking with you."

"Fine. What is it?"

Rebecca shivered a little from the cold and rain. "David, have I done something wrong that you have been avoiding me for the past couple of days?" David tried to dodge the question. "What are you talking about? There isn't anything wrong with me."

But Rebecca could tell that he was not being honest with her. "Tell me what you think of me."

David was surprised at the question. He loved Rebecca but knew that Adam would be better for her. Plus, he didn't want to ruin the friendship they both shared. "It doesn't matter what I think."

"But it does. Look..." David did not let Rebecca finish her sentence. He gave her one last look and started to walk inside. "But it does matter because I love you."

David stopped. Rebecca was so shocked at what she had said that she covered her mouth with her hands. David put his head down. He didn't even look at her. "That may be what you feel, but I don't share your feelings. I'm sorry but I don't love you."

His words were so hurtful. Rebecca felt like a piece of paper that was just ripped in half. The scenario kept repeating itself in her mind. She couldn't believe what she had just done. Rebecca started to cry. *I ruined everything. He hates me now. He hates me.*

"David. Wait. David..." Rebecca's voice trailed off. Her vision got blurry and she fell to the ground. David heard the thump and turned around. He saw Rebecca on the ground, getting soaked, and he ran to her. "Becky, Becky wake up. What have I done?" David placed his cold wet hand on Rebecca's forehead. "She's burning up."

David picked Rebecca up in his arms and then took her inside his apartment to call the doctor. He gave Rebecca an injection and told David that she became ill from being stressed and standing in the rain. He told David not to worry and that she would feel fine in about three days. After the doctor was gone, David tended to Rebecca.

He changed her out of her wet clothes and put one of his baggy T-shirts on her. He put his blankets on her, and put a wet towel cloth on her forehead. He kneeled down beside the bed and held her hand. He kissed her and then went to sleep beside her. *I love you too, Rebecca. I am so sorry. I will always love you.*

CHAPTER 3

The Shadow Man watched silently as Julie walked into the library. *Great. My next target has arrived. You thought the death of your friend Kristen was bad, wait 'till you see Julie's death. She will be such a mess that you won't even recognize her!* The Shadow Man laughed and then headed into the library after Julie.

Julie was working quietly on her science project, gathering facts about genetics and engineering. She was not enjoying this topic and she felt like she was the only person there. The library was empty, except for the librarian and a few other students. She got up and went in search of another book, while the Shadow Man loomed in the darkness.

In his hand he clenched a meat clever. *Take a slice out of life Julie.* She started to get frustrated, unable to find the book she was looking for. *Great.* Julie turned around and started to walk back to her desk, completely fed up.

Rebecca opened her eyes and noticed that her whole body felt heavy. Her eyes shut and suddenly, she knew she was dreaming. The phone began to ring off the hook at David's. He picked it up and answered, "Hello." The voice on the other side began to speak. It was Adam. "Hi David, it's Adam calling from the station. You and Rebecca better get over here right away. It seems we have some witnesses that say that they all saw a man dressed in a black coat holding a knife, following Rebecca, and all the murders seem to happen to her friends. I think she's being stalked by someone who doesn't like her."

David got up. *That would explain the auditorium, the elevator, and even the murders. But who would do something like this?* "I'll be right there but Rebecca is a little too sick to go anywhere. Adam, did you find out about the auditorium stage?"

"Yes, it seems there were a ton of termites nibbling at the stage and when the sandbags fell, the stage was too weak."

David got his answer. *Someone did all that on purpose. He looked at Rebecca. But who?* "Okay, thanks." David got his car keys, wrote Rebecca a note and then telephoned Cathy and asked her to come look after Rebecca while he went to the police station.

Rebecca tried to get up again. *This dream feels too real. David is taking to Adam, but it can't be.* She fell back into her dream.

The librarian stepped out to go next door and get some coffee, and left Julie alone in the library. Her way of accepting tragedy had always been to preoccupy herself. She would always do this when she was upset, or on the verge of crying her heart out. Even though she didn't like Kristen, she felt very bad about her death. Tears began to emerge from her eyes.

A noise made Julie sit up straight in her seat. It sounded like footsteps. Julie stood up. She did not scare easily, so she simply took out her pepper spray and walked in the direction of the sound. As she stood between the large shelves of books, the Shadow Man grinned.

"The girl who absorbs herself in books, should be absorbed by the books." His voice was cruel and raspy, as he pushed the shelf of books down, creating a domino effect with the other shelves. Julie ran out of her isle just before the books fell on her, and saw a message written on the wall.

"I am so sorry. I don't have anything against you and your friends, I just want Rebecca, that's all."

What Rebecca? The campus murders, all victims knew Rebecca. Got to warn her. Julie counted to three and then made a run for it out the main entrance of the door. Unfortunately, the Shadow Man intercepted her and she slipped and fell. When she looked up, she saw a man dressed in a black coat. His face was covered and he had a meat clever in his hand.

The man looked like evil personified. Julie fumbled with her pepper spray and finally sprayed it in her attacker's face. The Shadow Man was temporarily blinded, giving her enough time to run out of the library and into the street leading to David's apartment building. The Shadow Man bolted out of the library and walked towards David's as well. *Someone is going to die today.*

Julie never made it to David's house. As she turned the corner, the Shadow Man rammed her in the head, and she collapsed. He picked up her limp body and walked back to the library.

Rebecca dreamed that David was going to go to the station to talk to Adam. David sat patiently in Adam's office, although he did not really like Adam at all. Maybe it was because he was a little jealous that Adam and Rebecca went out. But the recent phone call had him worried. *So Rebecca is getting stalked. Then that means that technically I saved her last week. If I hadn't turned the corner when I did then Rebecca would be dead.*

I wonder who the hell this psycho is. At least Rebecca's safe. Cathy will take good care of her. Cathy sort of reminds me of Jen. Gosh, I haven't seen her in four years. Jennifer Carpenter. Jen was David and Rebecca's best friend in the whole entire world. Jen lived in New York with her boyfriend. She was a cool gal. She lived with her parents and her friend Malicine.

Maybe I should give Jen a call and ask her to come visit. David continued on, thinking of all his friends that he had not seen in a while.

At the library, Jeremy and Lana discovered the fallen bookshelves, and Julie's books scattered all over the floor. Jeremy looked at Lana.

"I hope Jules is okay."

She looked all around. "Oh my God. Look!" Jeremy followed Lana's finger. There they saw Julie lying on the floor with blood pouring out of a large cut on her head. *Someone must have knocked the bookshelves down and Julie must have got hurt.*

They hurriedly left the library with Julie and got into the car and drove to the hospital. Now it was Julie's turn to dream. In her dream she was still trying to get away from the Shadow Man.

She darted to the back of the building, thinking that the fire escape was the only way up without the Shadow Man finding her. She jumped, and jumped until she finally got a hold of the ladder. She struggled a bit at first but then managed to climb it. The Shadow Man saw her, but instead of going after her, he entered the building and got into the elevator.

Cathy sat in the dark living room all by herself. Rebecca's fever was still very high but she had gained conciousness. Cathy spread her long legs across the sofa. Her hair rested against the seat. As usual she wore her tights and a tank top. Rebecca always told her how envious she was of her because she could wear stuff like that. Rebecca could have dressed like that as well, but she was too shy about it.

I wonder if Rebecca is okay? Maybe I should check on her. Cathy got up and left to go check on her and she woke up. Her eyes barley opened. Her fever was still high but she knew that she was going to get better. A tear began to run out of her eye. David had rejected her. *How stupid of me to confess how I felt. Now he hates me.* Rebecca got herself up out of her bed and wobbled to the door.

A sudden pain in her head made her fall to the floor. "Oh no, not again." Rebecca could feel the strange sensations take over her body, and an image of three girls running away from a man wearing a black coat came into her mind. The man looked familiar. *Now where have I seen him before?* He held a meat clever in his hand. She would have continued the vision, but Cathy walked into the room. She saw Rebecca out of the bed and became upset.

"And what do we think we are doing? Get back in that bed."

Rebecca shook her head, as if she was pleading with Cathy, but she would not take no for an answer. A crash in the living room made them both jump. They looked at each other, hurried to the living room and found Julie there. She was very disheveled and had scratches all over her legs.

"Julie, what the happened to you? How did you get in?"

"There's no time to talk. The guy who is stalking Rebecca, he's here in the building. He tried to kill me tonight at the library but I got away. Call David."

Cathy ran to the phone but the line was dead. "The phone is dead! What are we going to do?" Rebecca was still groggy. *There's someone stalking me. Who would want to stalk me? I am not even worthy of being stalked.* There was a knock at the door and all three girls turned around, with fear on their faces. All except Rebecca - she was too sick to have a face of fear.

The knocking got louder, so Cathy went to the door and looked through the key whole. A girl stood in the doorway - a familiar looking girl. Cathy hesitated and then opened the door. Rebecca almost fell over. It was Jen. She was so happy that she wobbled herself to her and gave her best friend a hug.

Jen was surprised to see Rebecca at David's house. "Oh Jen. I missed you. Why are here? There's a man stalking me. He's here in the building. He wants to kill me. So how's everyone in New York. Jen I am so glad your back." Rebecca rambled on and on until she fell over. Cathy ran over to her and caught her before she hit the ground.

"What happened to her? Where's David? And what was she talking about?"

Cathy locked the door and told Jen about the terrible events that had taken place. She was shocked to hear such news, but she was prepared if there was an intruder - she had taken kickboxing and judo. Cathy put Rebecca back into the bedroom and shut the door. Julie, Jen and Cathy sat in the living room and discussed everything. They were going to wait for David to come home. They figured that the stalker might be in the building, but he didn't know which floor they were on.

Rebecca slept peacefully in her bed, as the closet door opened. The Shadow Man came out carrying a single red rose that had been dipped in fresh blood. He walked over to Rebecca and put the rose on her chest. Then he took off his coat and lay in the bed next to her. *Oh the bittersweet memories.* He turned to face her. His hand started to explore her.

Rebecca continued to sleep. He caressed her thigh and kissed her neck with a kiss like a spider bite. His tongue caressed her neck. He then lowered his eyes on her voluptuous body. His mouth went upon hers. His hidden passion for her poured out. Rebecca twitched a little and then started to make noises. Cathy heard her and decided to check on Rebecca.

The Shadow Man put his coat back on and went back into the closet. Cathy came into the room, and saw that Rebecca was sleeping. Cathy looked distressed, but she turned and went back into the living room. The Shadow Man grabbed a harpoon that was lying in the closet.

"Time to go fishing. Slut Kabobs, anyone?"

The Shadow Man snuck out of the room and walked slowly to where the girls were sitting. He saw Jen and then backed up. *Why is she here? Well, there's always room for one more.* David suddenly had an uneasy feeling so he and Adam raced to the apartment.

Rebecca woke up feeling somehow energized. She decided to take a shower, so she grabbed a towel and went to the bathroom. Jen was surprised at what Cathy and Julie told her, and she was shocked by the news that Kristen was dead.

"Look, I didn't like the girl anyhow, but still I feel bad for her. Who the hell would do something like that anyway? I would love to punch him in the face."

Julie smiled at Jen's wording. Jen turned her eyes and saw a shadow of a manly figure. Jen made a face at Julie. Julie eyed the corner to where the hallway was. Cathy didn't understand her until she saw the shadow as well. All three girls got up slowly and then ran to the kitchen.

The Shadow Man walked slowly towards the kitchen as well. He entered with the harpoon in his hand, but the girls were nowhere to be seen. *Strange.* He walked slowly like a tiger searching for his prey. Julie hid behind the closet where the ironing board was. Jen had a piece of two by four in her hand. Cathy had some knitting needles in her hand. They were the only weapons that they could grab.

Cathy heard Rebecca come out into the living room. *Shit!* Cathy slowly crept around the back entrance and tiptoed into the room. Rebecca just blankly looked at her. Cathy put her hand on Rebecca's mouth and whispered to her that the Shadow Man was in the room. Rebecca panicked. She didn't know what to do.

The Shadow Man saw Julie's feet behind the closet, so he raised his harpoon and threw it. It went right through the closet door and blood fell to the floor. Then, Julie fell to the floor as well. Jen came out of nowhere and smashed the Shadow Man in his head. Julie got up and kicked the Shadow Man in his stomach. All the girls started screaming as the Shadow Man got up again and started to walk out to the living room where Rebecca was...

Julie suddenly awoke. Her head hurt. Jeremy told her how they had found her, but she had no idea what had happened. All she wanted to do was to go and see if Rebecca was all right.

Rebecca was still dreaming, somehow connected to Julie's dream. Rebecca continued Julie's nightmare. The Shadow Man walked up to Rebecca. He placed his hand on her face and began to caress it. She was so frightened that she couldn't move. The Shadow Man grabbed her neck and began to choke her.

An alarm clock began to ring. Rebecca twitched her eyes and woke up with a scream. David rushed to her side. "Are you okay?

You feeling better?" Rebecca looked all around the house. "Where's Cathy and Julie and Jen?" David looked at Rebecca.

"Cathy left this morning. Julie had a little accident at the library and Jen isn't here. I think you had another nightmare."

Rebecca started to cry. *It was another nightmare that's all. Nothing else but a nightmare. Thank god. But what happened last night with David wasn't a nightmare. He did say that he didn't love me.* David saw the distress in Rebecca's eyes and he sat on the bed and gave her a big hug.

"Hey, about last night. I only said that because I was jealous about you and Adam. But when you told me how you really felt I didn't know what to say so I said whatever came to mind. Rebecca, I really like you as well. I love you. I have loved you ever since you and I became friends. I'll never leave you again."

Before Rebecca could respond David planted a passionate kiss on her lips. Rebecca was swept away by his passion for her. *Oh David. I love you.* Then, Julie, Cathy and Lana interrupted the special moment. "Um, guys. If you guys don't get ready for English class Mr. Hiller is going to kill you."

Rebecca and David smiled in embarrassment and then got up. Her fever had gone down and she felt a lot better. *Julie had an accident. I wonder what happened to her. I hope it wasn't what I was dreaming. But that can't happen. No way.*

"Julie, what happened to you at the library?" Julie studied Rebecca. *If I tell her she will just get worried about me but maybe I should. No, Rebecca has just finished recovering from a bad fever so I'll wait to tell her.* "Nothing really, a stack of books fell on me that's all. Someone accidentally had knocked the shelf down. I'm okay." Rebecca looked at Julie. *Coincidence. Maybe.*

"Wait. David, you said that Cathy was here with me all night. Why?"

David thought for a moment and then remembered, "You got

sick and I got called to take over someone else's night shift at work. Cathy offered to come and watch you. I am glad that she did." David smiled at Rebecca. Rebecca turned red. The group got their stuff and left the apartment. A dark shadow emerged from the closet. The Shadow Man held Rebecca's timetable. *Let's see if the true you has finally come back.*

The Shadow Man left.

Rebecca thought she was going to get bored out of her mind. Mr. Hiller wasn't in, as usual. Mr. Hiller was such a good professor. Rebecca smiled to herself. Actually, she used to have a big crush on him when she first arrived at the college, but now she simply respected him as a professor.

Mr. Lindale was the supply for their class today and Julie was blushing, since she had a crush on him. Little did she know, he also had a crush on her. Rebecca looked at him. *I guess he is handsome. He has a good body. Nice face. Great smile. His eye color was an exotic violet/yellow. Very attractive. Okay, I guess. Julie seemed to like him.*

"Good afternoon class. Your professor, Mr. Hiller, will not be in this week because he is sick. I will be supplying this class all week. Toady we are all going to the library for research on the ISU projects that Mr. Hiller assigned all of you guys."

Everyone grabbed their stuff and headed towards the library. *Oh, I totally forgot about the stupid ISU project. Well, it can't be that hard. All I have to do is check out a whole bunch of old papers and microfiche and pick an interesting story, write about it, present it and then hand it in. I can do that.* Rebecca was not pleased with the group she was assigned to, since she didn't know anyone in it except David and Julie.

The others in her group were Fred, Leana, Tracy and the guy she never wanted to see again - Keith Richards - Rebecca's ex boyfriend - the king of slim.

Rebecca felt awkward sitting in a group with Keith there. She had broken up with him over a month ago, but she still felt weird being around him. She knew she was being silly, since she was the one who broke up with him. Rebecca did not like him anymore, as a boyfriend, friend, or even a person.

What the hell's her problem? Keith wondered this while he watched Rebecca fidget in her seat. David could tell that there was some tension between the two. Rebecca gave David a smile. Everyone turned around to face Mr. Lindale. He was going to explain the ISU and then let everyone meet with their groups and discuss what topics they were going to choose.

"Today class, I do not want to be called Mr. Lindale because I am very close to your age and I do have a first name like all of you. My name is Jonathan, so call me that instead. Okay, the agenda for today is, you must all individually find a case or a story in the old papers and records that interests you. Then you must do more research on the case, story, or whatever you choose. Make a report on it and then you will all get into your groups, discuss what you found, and then present it to the class. Not today though, maybe late next week. All right class, move it!"

The class got up and scattered around the library. *Where to start?* Rebecca got up from her seat and then walked into the microfiche room. Miss Peterson was assisting others in the room, and there was one more machine left. Miss. Peterson turned around and saw Rebecca waiting patiently.

"What can I do for you dear?"

Rebecca couldn't help but smile. *Miss Peterson has always been the maternal one of the school.* "Well, actually, I have an ISU project and I was wondering if I could use that machine over there. I wanted to check out old newspaper reports from the 40's and 70's, if that's not a problem, of course."

Miss Peterson looked at her. Then she smiled, made Rebecca sit in the empty chair where the machine was that she was going to be using and scooted off to the back room where all the microfiche were hidden from students' eyes. A little while latter Miss Peterson arrived carrying four rows of microfiche. She planted them on the spare desk beside Rebecca's machine and left. She knew that Rebecca could manage by herself.

Rebecca grabbed the microfiche entitled March 2,3, 4 and 5th, 1947 and plopped it into the machine. She turned on her light, got the picture in on focus and then began to search for an interesting story. She had no idea what she was looking for, so she just skimmed through the many interesting articles until…

Rebecca's eyes nearly came out of their sockets. There, in front of her, was the article from her nightmare about a girl who had died, just like Tanya had died. *Maybe the article was about Tanya's murder, but that can't be. That is only a nightmare. Tanya Annabella Arkenson does not exist.* But the picture of the girl seemed to resemble her in a weird way. *Could it be? And if it is, then I have been right all along. Oh my God. Kristen!* Rebecca suddenly remembered that she had a feeling that someone she knew was in trouble, but she had no idea whom. She also remembered the horrible visions she saw at Kristen's murder scene. *Can it be? Can it be that what I saw did happen? Then that means that this whole Tanya thing is real and that also means that there is really a Shadow Stalker. That's silly. There is no Shadow Stalker. Only some crazy psycho killer but then why is it that so many bad things are happening to me?*

I have to print this out and show it to the others. Rebecca put her money into the machine and printed as much as she could find. This was evidence that she wasn't going crazy, or mad and that her dreams and nightmares of the Shadow Man were not just a hallucination. But then again, she had no proof that the Shadow Man was the real murderer. *Could he actually exist?*

Rebecca grabbed her stuff and ran out of the microfiche room.

She stood in the middle of the library and scanned the room in search of a familiar face. But instead, from the corner of her eye, she spotted an image of a dark shadow lurking against the wall. She motioned herself to the back of the aisle, in which she walked around the back towards where she saw the shadow. A man dressed in black stood in the middle of the isle, looking for Rebecca.

Rebecca took out a book from the shelf and rammed it in the man's face. He turned around, startled, but couldn't quite comprehend what was happening. Rebecca kept on hitting him with the book.

"What the hell do you think you are doing you idiot. It's me, Rebecca. Keith."

Keith. Rebecca stopped hitting him and pulled herself back a few steps. *Maybe he is the one who has been stalking me. Maybe he has something to do with all the mysterious accidents that I have been having.* She didn't even want to stand there and look at him, still very upset with him after what he did to her. He cheated with one of her friends, while he was dating her. He was sneaking around with Kristen. *Wait. Kristen.*

"It was you. You killed Kristen didn't you? It had to be you. You hated her after she told me the truth about you. You did say that you would get her back and now she's dead. Coincidence? I think not."

"Wait a, minute. I didn't kill Kristen. What the hell. I know you hate me, but to accuse me of that is just ridiculous. Your just still pissed off that I cheated with Kristen. You just need someone to blame. Look, I didn't want to fight with you; all I wanted is us to be friends again. Can we be friends?"

Rebecca made a face of anger. "Friends, you want to be my friend? I hate you Keith. I told you that not in a million years would we ever be friends again after what you did. There's no way you can ever make me your friend again. Never."

Rebecca stormed off back to her group. The research time had just finished anyway. She was furious and yet frightened by what she had just found out. If there was really a Tanya and she was murdered then why was she haunting Rebecca's dreams? She didn't know why, but she swore to find her killer and make him pay for what he had done - the crime that he got away with.

David, Julie, Keith, Tracy, and Fred were now sitting in their little research group. Rebecca couldn't wait so she told David and Julie to tell the others to meet her at the cafeteria in about ten minutes. She asked if she could be excused and left the library. She was determined to find the answers that would reassure her that everything that she was thinking wasn't just her imagination. The person who could help her clear up the thoughts was none other then Adam.

David looked at Julie. He had no idea what Rebecca was up to but he could tell she was pretty worried, and he gave Keith an angry glare. Keith saw David's glare, but he also saw a piece of paper that Rebecca had dropped, so he picked it up.

"Girl at the age of eighteen died last night. Her body was discovered this morning by Officer Corel. The young girl's name has not been released. The locals are very saddened by this discovery, particularly those who were close to her." Keith looked at Tanya's photo. The picture of the girl looked like Rebecca, with only a few small differences. *This is really warped.* The picture of Tanya's friends made Keith jump out of his seat. There in the middle of her friends stood a familiar face. A face he had seen many times before. A face he recognized.

Keith left the library in search of Rebecca. Maybe she would like to know the discovery he had made from her article. He spotted her heading to her car. He knew that she only had a driving permit, and not her full license, but she got into her car. She was known to break a few rules every now and then. So he watched her until she drove out of the parking lot, ran to his car and followed her. *I wonder where she's going?* Rebecca stopped in front of the police station. She parked her car, got out and ran into the police station. Keith parked his car to the side and waited silently.

Rebecca sat in Adam's office and waited for him to arrive from a meeting. She had a few minutes to wait, so she took out her binder and started to look at the articles.

She continued to read the articles until Adam finally arrived. He was surprised to see her, especially after they had called it quits. She gave Adam a big hug and then they both sat down. Rebecca told him everything that was happening to her.

Keith got bored waiting so he turned on his radio, closed his eyes and began to remember what happened that awful night when he and Rebecca broke up. She was at Cathy's that night. He had Kristen waiting in his car parked downstairs. He was trying to get Rebecca to come with him to the dance but she was mad at him and refused to go, so he took off with Kristen instead. They ended up getting drunk, and parked in an abandoned parking lot.

The intense heat fogged the windows. Keith and Kristen were all over each other, their naked flesh colliding with such force that the whole car shook. They both felt the forbidden passion and knew that what they were doing was wrong, but at that moment they just didn't care. In the meantime, Rebecca and Cathy had decided to go for a walk. That's when Cathy spotted Keith's car.

"Rebecca, isn't that Keith's car?"

Rebecca looked to where she was pointing and then stormed up to the car. She couldn't see easily inside the foggy windows, so she put her face right up against one, only to see a hurtful sight. Keith was on top of Kristen. Keith was all over Kristen! She was shocked. She was so mad that she took off her high heel and smashed his window, startling the lovers inside. Keith was shocked to see Rebecca. Right then and there, Rebecca told him that their relationship was through.

Keith suddenly woke. *That was a big mistake,* he thought. *I shouldn't have done that. It wasn't fair to Rebecca, Kristen or even myself.* Rebecca came running out with Adam from the police station. Keith's eyes perked up. *What the hell? Where is she running off to in such a rush?* Adam sat in the driver's seat of Rebecca's car, and she got into the passenger's seat. *Something big must be going on.* Keith started his engine.

"So Adam, what you are saying is that the stage at the auditorium was contaminated with termites? I bet the murders are linked somehow. There have just been to many strange accidents."

Keith started his car and drove to Rebecca's car, shivering a bit from the cold draft coming from within his car. He ignored his feeling and continued to drive. Adam looked into the rear view mirror to see Keith behind them. He froze when he saw a dark cloaked figure rise up from behind the seat in Keith's car.

Adam blinked his eyes and looked in the mirror again. Nothing. There was nothing there. He breathed a sigh of relief and drove off. The figure loomed out of the seat again. In his hand he held an axe. Keith drove peacefully down the street and decided to take a short cut down the alleyway. He heard a scathing sound behind him, so he turned to look, and saw the Shadow Man holding an axe. The axe came down and struck his neck.

Blood poured everywhere and the car crashed into a wall. The Shadow Man jumped out, his voice echoing throughout the alleyway.

"Nothing against you, but I couldn't let you tell Rebecca where you have seen me before. It would ruin the surprise for her when I tell her myself."

The Shadow Man walked back towards campus, a few feet ahead. Rebecca and Adam walked into the cafeteria, and found the others. She explained to all of them about her suspicions, even though she really did not want to believe. First the stage, then Kristen's murder and now... Maybe the killer was someone she knew, but who? Could this killer somehow be linked to the nightmares that she was having?

David and the other made a face and laughed at her. Julie, of course, did not. Even though she knew someone attacked her, she couldn't help but wonder if what Rebecca was saying made any sense. *If it did, it would explain a lot. Like Rebecca's constant nightmares, the accidents and Kristen's murder. Not to mention my attack. I hope that Rebecca is wrong because if she isn't then someone else is going to be attacked and it could be any of us.*

Rebecca was a little upset that no one really believed her, but she couldn't blame them because frankly, she didn't know what to believe. But, she had noticed that Julie was not laughing. The Shadow Man watched as she got up and left. An evil smile spread across his face. He knew what to do next. He had already chosen his next victim - Cathy.

CHAPTER 4

Rebecca knew that she was dreaming because she was wearing Tanya's white silk dress - another nightmare. She was dancing in a big ballroom with thousands of guests all dressed up in beautiful clothing. Everyone looked great. This dream was much like the previous one, but this time it was somehow very different. This time Jack was her date.

Rebecca was mesmerized with Jack's handsome appearance. She had never seen such a handsome man before, excluding her David, of course. He held her against his chest, and she turned red with embarrassment. She felt a sexual longing for him again. *No. No. I must stop this urge to have him. First of all he is not real and this is not right. He is Tanya's man and I am not Tanya. I must focus my attention on the crowd. I must keep a look out for the Shadow Man. I know he is here waiting for me somewhere. Waiting.*

Rebecca kept dancing around and around. Her elegance and grace made her the center of attention with all the guests. Jack smiled as he danced with his love. Rebecca got tired and asked Jack if she could take a little break, and go to the washroom. He escorted her to the entrance of the bathroom and then, like a gentleman, waited outside the door. Rebecca walked inside the bathroom.

There was no one else in the bathroom. Rebecca went into a stall and sat down on the toilet. All she wanted to do was close her eyes and relax. A shadow appeared on the floor, and Rebecca opened her eyes and noticed it. Her door was locked, and so were all the other doors to the stalls. Rebecca stood on top of her toilet, and peaked through the crack from the door. All she could make out was a shadow of a man.

She wasn't sure of who it was. The man took out a crowbar, and gripped it firmly. His voice was faint and evil. "Come out, come out where ever you are? Don't make this harder on yourself than it has to be."

It's the Shadow Man! Rebecca slowly took out a can of aerosol hair spray and a box of matches from her purse. She slowly lit the match and held the aerosol can away from the match. Just then, the Shadow Man rammed the door to the first stall. Then he proceeded to the second and then, last but not least, the third. He rammed the door open. Rebecca sprayed the aerosol towards the lit match, and a flame came towards the Shadow Man's face and burned it. He dropped his weapon and ran towards the sink.

Rebecca leaped out of the stall and ran towards the door. She continued to run, although she realized that she was in another dream. Suddenly, she found herself back in her own dorm room. There she saw Cathy sound asleep and Julie on the other bed, also sound asleep. They looked like little babies. She heard a knock at her door and opened it, but there was no one there.

Rebecca walked outside into the dark quiet hallway, still wearing Tanya's dress. She walked slowly down the hallway until she arrived at the entrance to the staircase where Kristen had died. She hesitated, but she finally opened the door to the entrance and walked through.

It was empty. Rebecca walked up the staircase and sat at the top of the stairs. She began to cry for her dear departed friend. *Oh Kristen. I wish I was here for you. I wish it would have been me instead of you. Wait.*

Rebecca stood up. Now it was all starting to make sense. *So many accidents and when the elevator fell I thought I saw someone, or something and the same goes for when I fell through the stage. I think I am being stalked. But that's silly, who would do something like that?*

She walked down the stairs and back to her room when suddenly, a hand grabbed her shoulder. She yelped as she turned around to face Jack.

"Jack, what are you doing here? You should not be here."

He looked at Rebecca. "I know but I must warn you Rebecca. You must be warned. He is after you again. You have to remember. You must remember who you were…"

Rebecca just stared at him blankly. *What is he saying? I think he's gone mad but wait.* She could tell by the look in his eyes that this was not a lie. She heard a noise and when she looked back, Jack was gone.

She felt a hand caress her neck. *It must be Jack.* She closed her eyes. The hand ran down her back and around her waist. She turned around, her eyes still closed, and her lips parted as she kissed Jack. The kiss was wonderful, but somehow different.

Rebecca opened her eyes and saw that the man she was kissing was not Jack - it was the Shadow Man. She backed away, as the Shadow Man took out his knife. She started to run, but she slipped, and before she could get up, she felt a sting on her arm.

When she looked at her arm she saw a long cut where blood started to ooze out. The Shadow Man smiled to himself. Rebecca got up, ran to her room and began to scream. Cathy and Julie woke up from their sleep.

Rebecca was thrashing around in her bed and both girls ran to her, trying to wake her up. Cathy grabbed her arm. Julie grabbed the glass of water that was beside the bed and splashed water on her face. She woke up with a shout, and looked at both of them in shock, sweat dripping down her forehead. The dream she had just had, seemed almost too real, even though she knew it was nothing more but one of her average nightmares.

"Rebecca, you practically scared us half to death. Are you all right?"

She nodded her head, and flinched. They noticed that there was blood all over her blanket. Rebecca could feel a pain in her arm, so she took the blanket off herself. Her arm was cut and blood was pouring out. She yelped in pain. Cathy hurriedly ran to the closet to get the first aid kit, and wrapped a bandage on her arm.

"Rebecca, that was a very big scratch. Almost too big for your nails to do something like that. Where did you cut yourself anyhow?"

Rebecca didn't even know. All she could remember was the Shadow Man - he had sliced at her arm in her dream. *It couldn't be. He isn't real. He is just a figment of my imagination.* While Cathy and Julie tended to Rebecca, the Shadow Man watched her from the closet. *Damn, too close. I almost finished her off.*

The Shadow Man raised his knife. Rebecca's blood dripped down the knife's blade. He had sliced her but didn't get to finish her off in time - she had surprised him by trying to burn his face with a match and a can of aerosol spray. *Next time. Next time we will meet face to face. By that time none of your friends will be left to stop me from killing you... again.*

Rebecca got up out of her bed and went to the bathroom to take a shower. She had to meet Bobby in the front of the campus in an hour. Today was her big day. Today she was going to take her driving test. *I hope I pass this time.* Bobby was her instructor, and what an instructor he was. He was in his mid twenties, had blond hair and blue eyes and when he wore his Wrangler jeans, he could break any girl's heart. He looked damn good in jeans and, lucky for Rebecca, he seemed to always be wearing them.

Rebecca got dressed, hurried to the front of the campus and saw that Bobby had not arrived yet. She looked at her watch. *He's late. As usual.* Then she saw two familiar looking faces.

"Hi Fred, Hi Leana."

She waved to the two she had met in her last English class. They were in her research group for her ISU projects. Leana noticed Rebecca and started to walk in her direction with Fred. Fred - he was the College sweetheart. He was short and cute, with a great smile. She always said that great things came in small packages, and there he was - Fred. The package. The great thing.

"Wuz up Rebecca?"

Rebecca smiled at Fred. She had heard a rumor that Fred had a crush on her, but she had no idea if it was true, or not. She had also heard that Fred and Leana were going out together. Leana also said hello. Rebecca was glad that she finally got to meet other people, and she wanted to make as many friends as she could. Fred kept on staring at her, and Rebecca caught him smiling sexily at her. She didn't know what to do.

Bobby pulled into the driveway. *Great. Just in time.* Bobby waved. Rebecca turned around to Fred and Leana. "Sorry guys. I have got to go. Drivers test."

"Good Luck."

Rebecca turned to face Fred. "Thank you Fred."

Fred watched her drive off. *No problem Rebecca. For you, anytime.* Fred walked off leaving Leana all by herself. Rebecca sat quietly beside Bobby who was wearing his jeans. *Cathy and Julie are going to want details.* She looked outside her window, and a vision flashed through her mind.

An image of a man holding an axe flashed before her eyes. The man was going to attack someone that she knew. She saw that it was the Shadow Man. *Stop it Rebecca Bailey. He is just a figment of your demented imagination. He does not exist.* The images in her mind ceased.

Bobby pulled over to the side and told Rebecca to trade seats with him. She was nervous, and she prayed to God to pass her test. She started the engine and began to drive slowly. *I hope Cathy is having better luck at her ambulance training then I am driving.*

Cathy sat alone in the ambulance. *It's so lonely here* she thought. Everyone else from her class had called in sick, and she seemed to be the only one there. She got up and walked in a circle around the ambulance until her instructor, Dexter Millstone, arrived.

"Cathy, are you the only one here today?"

She smiled. "Well, okay. Let's go train then. Shall we?"

She nodded her head and then got into the backseat of the ambulance. Dexter got into the driver's seat and drove off into the direction of Bakers Village.

Rebecca drove slowly and cautiously through Bakers Village. Her stomach began to growl and so Bobby told Rebecca to park the car beside the Sizzlin' Skillet restaurant.

"Congratulations Rebecca. You passed your test. Here, go in and buy some food for the both of us. I am hungry and I am sure you are as well."

Rebecca was shocked. "You mean it? I passed? I actually passed the test? I can officially drive. No way! Oh my God! Thank you Bobby."

Rebecca gave Bobby a big kiss and got out of the car and ran into the restaurant. All the pressure she had been on made her very hungry. Rebecca gave Bobby his food and waved goodbye to him. She went inside to telephone David and tell him the good news.

Cathy was bumped and tossed in the back of the ambulance until it finally it came to a stop. Dexter said he was going to take a short walk to go to the washroom. Cathy sat patiently.

Rebecca began to dial David's cell phone number when she suddenly had a strange feeling. Her head began to hurt and her eyes began to twitch. She fell to the floor and began to have a vision. She saw Cathy running away from a man, but it was not just any man, it was the Shadow Man. *Got to save her but I am so tired.*

Rebecca remained on the floor. Her eyes closed and she went to sleep but then she got up and started to walk in a zombie-like trance.

Rebecca began to sleep walk. She was trapped in a nightmare - a nightmare in which she had to save her friend. She saw an empty car with the keys still in it.

She plopped herself into the driver's seat and the drove off. *Where am I going? I don't even know where Cathy is? Follow your feelings Rebecca those will never betray you.* Rebecca followed her feelings. *Cathy is close by; I can feel her presence, and I can feel his presence.*

Dexter heard a noise and looked back. *Nothing*. He shook his head and continued to walk towards the ambulance. He stopped in his tracks, and looked back again. *Nothing*. He started to walk faster. As he put his hand against the door, the Shadow Man suddenly appeared behind him and strangled him with a wire. Dexter tried to free himself, but he couldn't.

The Shadow Man continued to strangle him, anger forming on his face. He started to pull on the wire harder and Dexter's lungs began to close. His face began to turn red and he couldn't breathe, or cough, or cry for help - all he could do was stare. He did manage to knock his fist against the ambulance. Cathy lifted her head, thinking that she heard a noise.

"Dexter?"

No response. She hesitated, but grabbed the handle of the door and began to pull it open. The Shadow Man raised Dexter off the ground and with one blow, broke his neck in half and let his body fall limply to the ground. Then he picked up the body, threw it to the front seat of the ambulance and got into the ambulance himself.

Cathy was about to open the door and get out when she heard the front door slam shut. "Dexter, is that you?"

The Shadow Man smiled. "Cathy, it's okay. I'm here. Sit down cause you are going to have the time of your life." Cathy smiled uncomfortably. *Dexter is sure acting weird. He is driving a little too fast.*

"Dexter. Slow down."

Dexter couldn't hear Cathy - he was dead. The Shadow Man smiled. *Finally, I will get rid of you Catherine. Finally.* The ambulance came to a halt, and Cathy fell to the floor, along with the medical supplies that had been neatly stacked inside the ambulance. She got up and ran for the door. *He's gone crazy!* She tried to open it, but it wouldn't budge.

I am trapped in here. Wait. What's that sound. Drip... drip... drip... I wonder what that sound is. Cathy walked towards the front of the ambulance just as a pool of blood began to flow inside. *Oh my god, he's dead. Dexter must have crashed into the window shield. I have to get out of here and get help.*

She grabbed a hammer and smashed the window of the ambulance, and managed to unlock the door. She ran out, only to see a trail of bloody footsteps which led to an alleyway. *Dexter's footprints. I should go and get help but I can't leave him.* Cathy walked towards the alleyway, following the footsteps, still holding the hammer in her hand. The alley led to a dead end.

"Dexter. Dexter where are you? Are you okay? Dexter speak to me."

Cathy felt a shiver run down her back, and she turned around and ran back to the ambulance. She opened the driver's side door and jumped in only to see Dexter's dead body limp in the passenger's seat. She screamed at the top of his lungs and jumped out of the ambulance, tears running down her cheeks. She ran to the back of the ambulance. *There's a radio! I can call for help!* She opened the back door and walked in.

Cathy failed to notice a shadow lurking behind her which crept up towards the back entrance of the ambulance. There, behind her, stood the Shadow Man, with a new weapon - a large needle full of poison. He walked up towards Cathy, who had her back to him. She stopped what she was doing when she saw the shadow of a man on the floor. She gulped - the killer was behind her. She gripped the hammer in her hand.

Please someone find me. Help me. Rebecca sped down the street, driving like a maniac. Scattered images flashed quickly through her mind - images of Cathy and the Shadow Man. *Got to get to her before he does.* Rebecca was about three minutes away from where the ambulance was parked. *I am going to save you Cathy even if it means I have to die trying.*

It took all of Cathy's effort to turn around and slam the hammer into the Shadow Man's face, but the force of the blow knocked him to the floor and knocked the needle out of his hand. Cathy screamed. *The guy who killed Kristen!* Cathy grabbed the fire extinguisher and used it against the Shadow Man. He hollered in pain. He was angry - he was going to make sure that Cathy died a horrible death.

Cathy noticed that the Shadow Man was in a puddle of water. The Shadow Man stood up with a hook in his hand. *I am going to gut you and play with your insides, bitch.* The Shadow Man slashed the hook at Cathy and she fell back. She noticed the electric heart booster. *Water... Booster... Water... Booster...* She knew what she had to do. She grabbed bottles of water and threw them onto the floor of the ambulance and outside to where the Shadow Man stood.

Cathy grabbed a hold of the two electric boosters. "You sick Bastard! You killed my friend and you've been placing my friends and me in danger! You are a crazy son of a bitch and I think you need some electroshock therapy!"

Cathy rammed the electric boosters against the water and a stream of electricity ran towards the Shadow Man. He was being electrocuted. Smoke started to emerge from his body, and he fell limp to the ground. *I hope he fries in hell.* Cathy was careful but she managed to leap out of the ambulance away from the puddle of water.

Cathy ran right into the street and in front of Rebecca's car, causing her to panic. "Oh, shit!" She steered the car away, nearly hitting

Cathy, and crashing the car. Her head smashed against the steering wheal.

Cathy ran to the car but was stopped in her tracks. The Shadow Man stood a few feet ahead of her. But she knew that she had to save Rebecca, so she ran in another direction. She ran and ran down the alleyway until she slipped. She looked around. *No one.*

Cathy got up but she was stunned when she felt a needle injecting into her arm. She opened her eyes wide to see who did it. The Shadow Man drove the needle hard into her arm, and she fell over in a deep sleep. He picked her up and took her back to the car where Rebecca still lay unconscious.

Hours later, Cathy and Rebecca awoke to find Bobby and Jonathan. Bobby was surprised to see that Rebecca had stolen his car and driven off when he stepped outside to go to the bathroom.

Jonathan was passing by when he had heard a car crash.

Cathy and Rebecca looked at each other. Cathy's arm was sore, but had no idea what happened to her. All she could remember was that she was running from someone. *But who?* Rebecca remembered that she was in the restaurant and she had a strange feeling and that's all she could remember. She did not remember how she ended up in Bobby's car.

Bobby and Jonathan decided that Rebecca must have been sleepwalking and that she had no idea what she was doing. Cathy told Jonathan about Dexter. Jonathan called the hospital in which Dexter worked for and they said that Dexter was out of town, and his ambulance was parked in the parking lot. Cathy was confused.

She didn't even notice that she was wearing normal clothes. But she could have sworn that she was wearing another uniform. Bobby and Jonathan looked at both the girls and said, "You two really need a lot of rest. You especially, Rebecca. We won't say anything about this if you don't."

Both girls agreed.

"Let's act like nothing happened, okay."

Jonathan took Cathy and Rebecca back home and Bobby called a tow truck for help. He didn't notice a man with a long bloody knife emerging out from the shadows. He turned around and was face to face with the Shadow Man. That was the last time Bobby ever saw the daylight.

Rebecca paced up and down the hallway of the empty reference room. Cathy was very shaken up. She said she was attacked, but there was no proof. Dexter was out of town and his ambulance was parked at the hospital. Rebecca didn't know what to believe, all she knew was that she ended up in a car and she had crashed it. Cathy told her that she thought that the guy who attacked her could have been the same man who killed Kristen. The killer was out there and Rebecca knew that there was something more to him than just Kristen and her friends. She knew that he had something to do with Tanya's murder, but how was he involved?

Rebecca went back to her room. Cathy was going to stay with Jeremy for a few days. Julie decided to go and stay with Lana. Rebecca decided she could use some quality time with herself. She wondered if she could somehow go into another one of Tanya's dreams, but for some reason she was beginning to think that maybe they were not dreams at all. Maybe it was a memory. But then, why would she be able to see it? Nevertheless, she was determined to see if she could drift off into another one of Tanya's dreams.

She put on the most comfortable gown that she owned and went to sleep. Her bed never felt so soft and comfortable before, and she slept soundly. A raspy and evil voice echoed through the bedroom and her eye fluttered opened. *What was that sound?* She slowly got out of bed.

Rebecca walked out of her bedroom. Victoria Grace opened her bedroom door. She thought that she heard a sound. Victoria saw Rebecca walk by her, looking like a zombie in a trance. Victoria figured that she must be sleepwalking, and she knew never to wake up a sleepwalker. *I better follow her and make sure that she does not hurt herself.*

Victoria ran to her closet to get her robe. When she came back, Rebecca was gone. "Now where did she go? I better go find her."

Victoria was also one of Rebecca's friends, but she really didn't have time to spend with the gang. Everyone liked her, but she had trouble making time for her friends. She was heiress to a lot of money, and she lived in a mansion with her stepfather. Her mother had passed away almost two years ago.

Victoria had long dark brown hair, hazel eyes and a gentle smile. A lot of people thought that she was a snob because she was so rich, but she wasn't. She was just a very rich young lady. She grabbed her flashlight and went out after Rebecca who roamed down the dark hallway of the school.

She was following the voice - the voice that called for her to come - the voice that she hadn't heard from in many, many years. She looked like an angel in an evil trance, wearing a white see through nightgown. Her hair was out and she looked as if she was filled with fury. She walked down the cold cobblestone steps, following the voice which seemed to be coming from the old campus.

The old campus had closed down many years ago. It was once a high school. Rebecca opened the door leading to the lower floor of the building. Slowly and cautiously, she took a step down the stairs. Victoria spotted her just as she closed the door.

"She's at the old campus. I have to make sure she doesn't get hurt."

She began to run to the door, but she ran right into her boyfriend and his friend.

"Hey, where the hell are you going at this time of night?"

Victoria looked up at her boyfriend. "Jared, Rebecca is sleepwalking. I have to follow her to make sure she doesn't hurt herself."

"Why don't you just wake her up?"

Victoria looked at Rick, who had just spoken. "Moron, you can't wake up a sleepwalker. It can be dangerous for them. Now, are you going to help me, or what?"

Jared looked at Rick. "Do we have a choice?"

Victoria smiled and nodded her head. The three of them then approached the tall dark building that Rebecca had entered. She was now standing in a room - a room in which she could hear the sound of dripping water. She strained her ears and she could still hear the voice whispering and taunting her name.

"Rebecca… Rebecca… Tanya… Tanya…"

She looked all around. She knew that she was dreaming but the campus looked a little too real. "I think that I have been here before. I remember. This is my old high school. Good old Harlond High. My locker number was 436. I remember everyone. Amy, Claudia, Daniel, Samantha, Wendy, Jack, Steven and Isabella. My friends. I wonder where they could be now?"

Rebecca was in a daze. Her mind was somehow stuck in a memory of Tanya's past. Rebecca pranced around like a ballerina. She walked to the locker that she remembered. She was so excited. She opened the locker and just stared at its contents.

"I don't remember putting that in my locker."

Victoria, Jared, and Rick walked down the steps. It was cold and smelled like old paint that was rotting from the walls. It seemed to have been abandoned for many years. The stairs were old and misshapen, and struck Jared as having no sense of aesthetics. Jared was also one of Rebecca's friends. He too had many things to do in his life, and although his friends were important to him, he hardly had any time to spend with them. That made him a very good match for Victoria.

"Hurry up. She could be anywhere down here. We have to find her."

Victoria liked Jared's friend Rick. He was a skinny guy with green eyes, a great smile and short black hair. She thought he was nice.

Victoria halted when she spotted Rebecca, looking frightened as she held one of the old lockers open. She seemed to be looking inside, but Victoria knew that was impossible because her eyes were closed. Rebecca stared in horror at the contents of her long forgotten locker.

The Shadow Man leaped out at her with a javelin in his hand. "You could never do javelin very well, so I have decided to teach you. Come here."

Rebecca screamed and began to run. Victoria heard the scream and quickly ran for her. She did not see the shadow that lurked around the corner, hungry and waiting. The others ran after Victoria. She slipped and fell down the remaining steps, and slammed her head against the wall and was knocked unconscience. Rick and Jared, were right behind her and also slipped and fell slamming their heads against the wall.

"Shit."

Jared grabbed Victoria and shook her. She moaned, opened her eyes and spoke softly. "Go and get Rebecca. I am fine."

Rick helped Victoria to her feet.

Jared smiled. He got up and walked towards where Rebecca stood screaming. The Shadow Man threw the javelin at her, but she jumped out of the way. The javelin landed right in between Rebecca and Jared. Of course, Rebecca could not see Jared, or the others because she was in a dream.

"Where did that thing come from?" Jared stood still. *Rebecca couldn't have thrown that javelin. Maybe this place is haunted.*

Jared looked back to see a figure of a man run off. Rebecca also ran off. Jared blinked his eyes. *That couldn't have been the… ghost. Could it? Never mind.* Rebecca screamed as she ran. She had to get away - she had to find shelter.

Rebecca ran down the abandoned hallway to a nearby staircase. *Perfect, I can hide there.* Rebecca walked towards the staircase with a sledgehammer in her hand. She knew that it would not take the Shadow Man long to find her. Rebecca slowly opened the door and saw that there was no one in sight, so she walked inside. The door creaked closed. She stood near the railing, looking down.

The Shadow Man watched her from the ceiling above, staring at her from the ventilation shaft above her head. He climbed down and landed right behind her. Her fear began to build up as she turned around. The Shadow Man grabbed her by her neck and began to strangle her.

The Shadow Man lifted her off her feet and the sledgehammer fell out of her hand, landing on the floor. Jared heard the loud bang and ran towards the staircase. He opened the door and saw the sledge hammer lying on the floor.

Where the hell is Rebecca? Jared had no idea that she was hanging right above him. The Shadow Man held her even higher and then, with a violent shake, let her go. Jared looked up in time to see her begin to fall towards the ground but she managed to grab the stair railing. Jared did not see the Shadow Man standing behind the railing.

He ran up the stairs. "Don't worry Rebecca, I'm coming to get you." He ran up the steps to where Rebecca was slipping. Before she let go of the rail, Jared grabbed her hand and pulled her back up. At this point he did not care if it was dangerous to wake up a sleepwalker; Rebecca was definately a danger to herself when she was asleep.

Jared shook Rebecca violently. "Wake up Rebecca! Snap out of it!"

Rebecca opened her eyes. She had no idea where she was. She looked into Jared's eyes, and he could tell that she was in confusion. Jared reassured her that everything was going to be all right. He then led her back to where Victoria and Rick were waiting. She was surprised to learn that she had been sleepwalking. *No wonder the night-*

mare felt so real.

Rebecca walked towards the cracked mirror that was on the wall and noticed some red marks on her neck that looked like strangulation marks. *It can't be. He couldn't have been there actually trying to kill me in my sleep. Could he?* Victoria, Rick and Jared did not notice the marks on her neck, and they walked her back to her room. The Shadow Man watched as all of them walked back to the dorms. *I almost had her. Almost. Looks like I need to shed some more blood to get my point around that they should leave this fight between her and me alone.* The Shadow Man left in a fury.

Rebecca sat near her window and watched the snowfall. November had almost come to an end. *I love the snow. Watching it makes me feel so calm.* She sat at her window and continued to watch the snow as it fell gracefully to the ground. This was the first time in many weeks that she felt calm, peaceful, and at ease - the first time in weeks that she felt free.

CHAPTER 5

The long weekend had finally arrived. *Yeah.* Rebecca was despondent. *It's not like I do anything for fun on the long weekend. I don't even go anywhere. Maybe it's because I don't have anyone to go with. I am just going to stay home and be bored. That will be great fun.* Rebecca got up and shook her head.

"Sarcasm really ain't your thing."

There was a knock at the door, so she walked over and answered it. In the doorway stood Victoria, and her boyfriend Jared. Rebecca smiled. She really missed these guys but they were too busy with other social engagements to socialize with her and the others.

"Well, well, well. What brings you two to my humble dorm room?"

Victoria and Jared both laughed. Rebecca made a gesture for the both of them to enter her room. Cathy and Julie had gone to the gym to work on the development of their perfect bodies, in order to make an impression on their men. Speaking of men, David had not phoned Rebecca after he heard bout her little sleepwalking incident from Jared. *I wonder where he is? I hope he isn't mad at me.*

Victoria stared at Rebecca. She could tell that she had been preoccupied and different for the last couple of days - ever since the sleepwalking incident. *I wonder what's wrong with her. She seems so distant.*

"Becky, are you sure that everything is all right with you? You seem a little distracted. Actually that's why Jared and I are here."

Rebecca looked up at Victoria. "I am inviting you to come stay the weekend with my friends at my house. It will be so much fun.

Everyone's going to be there."

Rebecca looked at her. *Did she just say her house? She didn't mean her house.* "Did you say your house Victoria?"

Victoria shook her head and Rebecca's jaw dropped open. "You mean the mansion. You're asking me to stay over the weekend at your mansion. Of course I am going to come. Wow, a mansion. This is going to be so cool. Maybe then I can tell you about all the horrible stuff that has been happening to me. I'm sure you weren't told how Kristen died."

Victoria and Jared both looked at Rebecca when she said that. "What do you mean by how Kristen died? Is there something that you know about her death that you aren't telling us?"

Rebecca didn't know what to say. All she could do was shake her head. She really wanted to tell them, but couldn't take a chance on getting them involved. She had already lost Kristen and she almost lost Cathy. *I bet that stalker of mine will come to the mansion. This time I'll be waiting and I'll be ready for him.*

Victoria and Jared both understood. They knew that she would tell them when she felt the time was right and she had a chance to finish grieving for Kristen. Victoria told her to pack her bags and wait at the campus parking lot at dusk. Rebecca walked the two outside and then returned to her room. *Well, I have to tell them sooner, or later. Better sooner then later.*

Rebecca got her suitcase out and began to pack with a smile on her face. *This is going to be fun. At least I hope so.* Rebecca waited until she saw Cathy, Julie, and David. She waved and ran up to them. "Hi guys. Hi dumbo."

David made a face at Rebecca and so did Cathy. *Oh no, not that stupid little flirtation, teasing game. God knows how many times I have done that with Jeremy for heavens sake. Talk about Jeremy, where the hell is he?* Cathy turned around, and saw Jeremy. Along with Jeremy was Jonathan, Leana and Fred. *How many people did*

Victoria invite? Oh yea, I forgot. We are all going to a mansion.

"Hey guys, wuz up?"

Rebecca looked at the others and noticed that Fred was among the men. *Great. Just great.* Fred looked at Rebecca and smiled. *Weirdo.* Rebecca rolled her eyes until she saw Victoria arrive with the rest of her gang of friends.

Victoria walked towards the others with Sarah and Jared. *Wait, that makes how many...let me see... that makes... one, two, three... that makes nine people in total. Wow.*

Victoria gave everyone a sheet of paper. *What's this?* Victoria whistled to get everyone's attention. "Thank you for coming here today. I am going to make sure that everyone has a great weekend. The paper that I have given you all is the itinerary for this long weekend. Be patient and the bus will be here to pick us up soon. Find a partner. Gosh I feel like a teacher."

Rebecca and the others started to laugh, and so did Victoria. Rebecca didn't really know all the people that were there. She didn't really know Sarah, Leana, or even Fred very well, but she really hoped that she would get to know them all very well on this weekend excursion.

Good, maybe I can make a few new friends. The bus finally arrived and everyone grabbed their belongings and got ready to board the bus. Cathy held Jeremy's hand and Julie held Jonathan's hand - today he wasn't a teacher, he was her boyfriend. David held Rebecca's hand and Jared kissed Victoria.

The Shadow Man watched as everyone got on the bus. *So many are going, so few will come back alive. I'll make sure of that.* The Shadow Man ran to the bus, but before anyone could see him, he crawled underneath the bus.

It was almost an hour before the bus arrived at Victoria's mansion estate. Rebecca's eyes opened wide when she saw the extravagant mansion, and her mind began to tingle. A sudden flash of

Tanya's house entered her mind. She blinked and the image disappeared. She turned to look at David who was sound asleep on her shoulder. She smiled and gave him a nudge. He awoke, yawned and rubbed his eyes, and looked at her with a smile.

Everyone was looking at Victoria's mansion. *Wow, if I had a house like this I would come home more often.* Rebecca was smiling, but she suddenly felt a terrible pain in her head. She got up from her seat and then suddenly fell asleep, landing on David. Victoria and the others got worried, but Rebecca was swept into a prophetic dream.

Rebecca was in a large living room with the whole gang. Out of the corner of her eye she saw the Shadow Man run by the window. *He's here. Oh my god. He's here.* Rebecca suddenly awoke to find herself still on the bus, with David staring at her..

"Hey, you okay? What happened?"

I can't worry them for nothing. It's not like my dreams are one hundred percent true. But I have this uneasy feeling. "Nothing. I felt a little dazed. I'm fine."

David looked at her strangely but let it drop. *Good. Well, if my stalker is here I am going to get him.* Victoria turned around to face Jared. She knew that there was something strange going on with Rebecca and she was determined to find out what it was.

The bus pulled into a large circular driveway and a red carpet was rolled to the entrance of the bus. A tall good-looking man, named Tony stood by the entrance of the mansion. Victoria told everyone to gather their stuff, and get off the bus. Rebecca was very excited. Everyone held their handbags and backpacks in their hands. Two elderly men carried everyone's luggage.

As Rebecca and the others walked towards the entrance of the mansion, she saw several various images in her mind - bodies, food, money, and, last but not least, the Shadow Man.

"Victoria. How's the security here, by the way?"

Victoria turned around and looked at Rebecca. *What an odd*

question. "Why?"

She shook her head. "Just curious I guess." David knew what she meant by her question, so he put his arm around her as they walked towards the door. He whispered in her ear that he would stay with her and take care of her. Rebecca looked into his eyes. *I really do love you David. I really do.*

Finally everyone was inside Victoria's mansion, and the door to the mansion shut. The Shadow Man crawled out from underneath the bus with a hook in his hand. He stood on the red carpeting.

"Now this is what I call a royal greeting. This long weekend is going to be a scream." He laughed and walked by the side of the mansion.

Everyone was led into the gigantic main hall. The walls were decorated with fine craftsmanship and everything was exquisite. Rebecca looked all around the hall until her eyes landed on an old woman who was staring at her. She started to feel uncomfortable with the woman's staring, so she narrowed her eyes and looked to the floor.

Victoria smiled and ran up to the woman, giving her a very big hug. "Everyone, welcome to my estate. I hope that your weekend will be a weekend to remember. This marvelous woman beside me is the woman I love the most. May I introduce my Aunt Stephanie Mystique, the world famous psychic, also known as Madame Mystique."

Everyone clapped their hands and started to hoot and whistled. *A psychic. Wow. Maybe she can help me figure out what is going on with me. But I won't ask her right now. Asking for something like that so fast would make me seem rude and uncivilized, and those are two things I am not.*

Plus, I don't believe in psychics anyway.

Victoria's aunt greeted all of the guests and Victoria announced that dinner would be served within the hour, so she told everyone to find someone to bunk with for a room. Cathy smiled at that idea. Her and Jeremy got their stuff and went to find the room that they were assigned. Julie and Jonathan also did the same. Everyone found a partner. David grabbed Rebecca's hand.

"Hey, shall we go find our room?"

David smiled at her. His smile had somehow made her blush. Rebecca knew what David had in mind. A long weekend; one bedroom; a lot of privacy; perfect opportunity. Rebecca smiled at his idea, and they found a room, after about ten minutes - the place was too big! David opened the door and walked in.

Rebecca thought that she was going to die. There was a king-size waterbed and a large dresser with drawers for their belongings. David started to laugh like a maniac. He had never been in such a prestigious place before. Rebecca ran to take a look at the bathroom, and all she could do was stare. David followed her in and did the same.

There was a built in sauna, a whirlpool, a Jacuzzi, a stand up shower and a home gym. Rebecca knew that her weekend was going to be fun. Especially since she had David to spend it with. David looked at Rebecca and started to growl. She grabbed a pillow from the bed and smacked him and he grabbed the other pillow and started to smack her. The feathers from the pillows flew everywhere.

David jumped and grabbed Rebecca. The force of his jump made her land right on top of the waterbed with him lying on top of her. Their eyes met. David's mouth hungrily went over her soft luscious lips. *He tastes so good*, Rebecca thought as their lips collided. David got up and then closed his door.

"How about some desert before dinner?"

Rebecca laughed a little. "Okay."

David growled like a tiger and then jumped back on the bed. Rebecca's screams could be heard throughout the hallway as he tickled her. David threw off his shirt and unzipped his pants. He planted himself firmly on her and then began to reveal what Rebecca was hidden beneath her soft cotton dress.

Rebecca and David would have kissed the night away but they suddenly remembered that they had to be back down in time for dinner. David crawled off of her and hurriedly began to change. Rebecca just watched in amazement as David stripped off his clothes. Finally, Rebecca got to have a great view of David's amazing body, and she felt like she was going to melt. When David finished dressing he looked at her.

"What? Why are you staring at me? Oh, I am not like you. I am not going to change in front of you. Only a male pig would do something like that. I am a mature woman."

David felt offended. "So I'm a pig and your Miss. Mature Woman. We will see about that."

David ran after Rebecca. He finally caught her and unzipped her out of her dress. His lips were busy caressing her skin as she quickly put on her dress. She didn't want to miss dinner. She was hungry.

"David, you can ravage me later. I have to eat before I participate in Body Olympics you know."

David laughed. "Body Olympics?"

She nodded her head and they headed downstairs. Rebecca looked for the others but none of them had arrived except for Leana and Fred. Fred looked really handsome in his suit, but not as handsome as David did. Leana looked okay in her evening gown dress. *I don't really like her that much. That's because I don't know her. Maybe I should go and mingle.*

"David, I am going to go and mingle."

David smiled at her and then she walked towards Leana and Fred. "Hey. You guys look great." Leana turned to look at the speaker. *Oh, her. Great.* Leana didn't like very many people. The only person she seemed to talk to was Fred. Leana was a very beautiful girl with light brown eyes and short brown and auburn hair, making her look like she was from Hawaii.

Fred was a handsome Spanish man. In fact, he was almost too handsome. He had short, spiked dirty blond hair and green eyes. He wore baggy clothes and his voice was soft and smooth. *Too bad he's attached to that girl. No offense and all, but Leana always seemed like she had another agenda.*

"Hello Rebecca. You look nice."

Rebecca smiled. Fred was a sweetheart. Rebecca heard laughter in the background. *Must be Victoria.* Rebecca turned to see the rest of the gang coming down the large staircase. Victoria looked gorgeous in her light green satin dress. She had her hair pinned up. Cathy looked very sophisticated in her silk evening gown. Julie, well she looked like herself, basically. She was wearing a normal long summer dress.

Jeremy and Jonathan were wearing tuxedos. All of them looked great. Sarah had finally arrived with Jared by her side. They were good friends. Rebecca noticed Julie and Cathy were very happy. *I wonder why?* Rebecca excused herself and walked over to them.

"Hi Becky. So, did you and David…?"

Rebecca blushed. "Actually, I was about to ask you two the same question. Did you guys, you know…?"

Cathy began to blush, but Julie just stood there like everything was normal. "Fine. Yes and no. Jeremy and I just made out that's all. Now you tell me what happened with you."

Rebecca smiled shyly. "Well, David and I kind of landed on the waterbed and we sort of, almost did, but we didn't have any time because we had to be here for dinner."

Cathy made a shocked expression on her face. "Face it Rebecca. You were hungry weren't you?"

Rebecca started to turn red. She quickly changed the topic to Julie. "So Julie, what happened with you?"

Julie just plainly looked at Cathy and Rebecca. "We did it." Rebecca and Cathy's face grew wide. "What do you mean? You guys really did it? Oh my God." Julie made a face of disgust. "What is with you two. I did it with him about three weeks ago. I just forgot to tell you, that's all."

Rebecca and Cathy were shocked. *That little sneak. She did it before we could do it with our men. I can't believe it.* Victoria waited about ten minutes more for everyone to arrive and then took them to the dining room. The food was set out on a large table. Victoria said it was like a buffet so that everybody got to pick and choose what they wanted to eat.

Rebecca sat in the corner of the large dining room wanting to see the first snowfall of winter by herself. The snow looked so beautiful as it fell down to the ground. Stephanie, Victoria's aunt noticed Rebecca sitting all by herself and decided to introduce herself.

"Hello dear, and you are…?"

Rebecca looked up at the woman. *Oh, it's Victoria's aunt.* "My name is Rebecca. Rebecca Bailey." Stephanie smiled. "Nice to meet you Rebecca. You already know who I am. I like it when people call me Madame Mystique."

Rebecca smiled. *Maybe I should ask her now.* "Madame Mystique, I was wondering if I could ask you a question?"

The psychic nodded her head, so Rebecca asked her about dreams and nightmares. Madame Mystique explained that a nightmare is nothing but fears and worries. She said that in order to get rid of nightmares, one should take a stand and face your fears. If this is done, the nightmares will stop.

Lucy, the young woman who did the cleaning of the house, was busy checking the bedrooms to make sure that everyone was properly settled. She had been working in the mansion for about three years and was almost the same age as Victoria, who was seventeen.

Lucy walked to the third floor in the south wing. She opened the door to Cathy and Jeremy's beautiful bedroom. Lucy smiled happily. It had been so long since they all had so many guests come over.

It got boring with no one to tend to.

Lucy noticed that the window was opened, so she walked over and shut it tight. Lucy was such a kind and loyal worker. It was her day off, but she still wanted to stay a bit and help the guests settle in before she left. Lucy finished checking the room and left to check the room that was across the hall.

The door was wide open. Lucy found this strange, so she peered inside the large, immaculate bedroom and saw that there was no one in sight. The bedroom was in perfect order, except that the television was on. She walked to the set to turn it off. She noticed that her favorite show was on. It was a soap opera called *In Our Days*. She sat down on the bed and started to watch her show.

A dark figure approached her from the closet beside the door. The door was locked tight, but Lucy didn't notice. In the mirror a reflection of the dark figure could be seen holding a hook - it was the Shadow Man. He raised his silver hook and positioned himself. *Aim to kill*, he told himself as he got ready to jab the hook into Lucy's skin.

Lucy felt a chill and turned around to see the Shadow Man behind her. "Once you get hooked, you always get hooked. I never miss this show either." Lucy did not even have time to blink her eyes as the hook came down and was jabbed into her chest. Blood spewed out of her mouth and down her eyes. There was nothing left but a blank expression on her face.

The Shadow Man let go of her and let her body fall to the ground. *Perfect*. Lucy's body was carried out of the room. The Shadow Man walked down the hallway. *Time to find another kill*. Rebecca suddenly flinched as a vision came into her mind. But then it faded. *Strange*. Madame Mystique told Rebecca about the town's annual carnival. Rebecca smiled - she loved carnivals.

Cathy and Jeremy were walking around in the large hallway of the upstairs. She smiled and asked Jeremy if he was tired and wanted to go to sleep. He smiled and led her to the bedroom. She went to the bathroom and then jumped into the bed with Jeremy. Everything was going great for the two, but Cathy felt something damp at her feet.

Cathy got up and threw over the blanket. There was a stain of blood on the spreadsheet. Cathy looked at Jeremy. Jeremy put his clothes back on and then searched the bedroom. There were no signs of anyone in the room. Cathy was frightened. A sudden drip... drip... drip... sound echoed throughout their room.

"What is that sound? Where is it coming from?"

Cathy looked all around the room. A drop of blood fell on her cheek. *Oh my God!* Jeremy and Cathy both looked up. The ceiling began to crumble and a familiar figure landed on the bed - Lucy. Cathy let out a scream and Jeremy ran to her and covered her eyes and hugged her. Cathy opened her eyes and saw a familiar man lurking in the shadows.

"Oh my God! It's him! He's here! Jeremy!"

Jeremy turned to see the Shadow Man standing against the wall with a machete in his hand. Blood dripped off of its blade. Cathy grabbed Jeremy's arm, but he was in shock. He had finally met Kristen's killer face to face - almost face to face - the Shadow Man's face could not be seen. Jeremy and Cathy both ran into the bathroom and locked the door.

"We have to find a way to get out of here."

Cathy turned around to find a telephone. *These rich people honestly.* Cathy grabbed the phone and began to dial David's cellular number. *Please pick up.* David's phone began to ring and he took it from his coat pocket and answered it.

"Hello."

"It's me Cathy. He's here. He's..."

The dial tone went dead and the lights in the mansion all went out. The Shadow Man shut down the circuit board for the entire mansion. He laughed at his handy work. Cathy kept on trying the phone but it didn't work. David was worried now. Cathy sounded hysterical on the phone. David turned to see if he could find Rebecca, but she had also disappeared.

Rebecca walked down the dark hallway of the mansion, feeling very afraid. *I have to find Cathy and Jeremy. For some reason I feel that they are in trouble. I want to see what they are doing.* Rebecca stopped in her tracks. The Shadow Man stood in front of her with blood dripping from his machete. Rebecca thought she must have been swept into another dream - another nightmare. The Shadow Man walked towards her and Rebecca closed her eyes. *He is not real. He is just in your dreams. He is not here. He is not here.* Rebecca opened her eyes but the Shadow Man kept on coming closer. She tried it once more. *He is not here. He is just a man from your nightmares.* Rebecca opened her eyes again, and the Shadow Man was gone.

Good. Thank God. Rebecca ran off in fear. The Shadow Man watched her leave. *I could have killed you, but first I want to kill your friends.* The Shadow Man walked in the direction from which Rebecca had come and found a young girl walking down the hall.

"Shit, I am lost. I think I should go back and find the others."

Sarah stood completely still. She heard a noise.

"What was that?"

Sarah whipped herself about.

Sarah saw an image of a man, and then she saw the shining of a blade. She screamed but the man grabbed her by the neck and threw her against a sharp pin.

The Shadow Man laughed and then proceeded back to Cathy and Jeremy's wing.

Cathy and Jeremy opened the door and crept outside to the hallway. The coast was clear. They walked towards the staircase, and then Cathy remembered that Rebecca had brought her cellular phone.

"Jeremy. Becky has her cell. Let's go get it. We can call the police for help."

Jeremy hesitated a little, but he did not want the Shadow Man to come back.

"Okay. Let's go."

They turned back and walked towards Rebecca's room, but the Shadow Man was not far behind. David walked into Cathy's bedroom, but there was no sign of either of them. The ceiling looked like it had caved in. He walked into the bathroom - nothing. *Maybe they both went back downstairs to get help.* David walked back down.

Leana and Fred walked to their bedroom. *What is the big deal? So there's a power failure. You would think that these rich snobs would have all that covered. But no.* Leana was pissed. Fred was worried about the others - so many had disappeared. *I wonder where they are.*

Victoria and Jared walked around the mansion hoping they would find someone, but they couldn't. Victoria noticed a trail of blood on the carpet so they followed it to the closet. When Jared opened the closet, Tony's body fell out and landed on him. Victoria started to scream when suddenly, a hand grabbed her shoulder. She whipped herself around and saw Rebecca.

"Why are you screaming?"

Rebecca followed Victoria's eyes to Jared and saw Tony. "Oh my God! Tony! Tony! Wait! That means he's here! He's here!"

Victoria looked at Rebecca and began to shake her. "Rebecca who is here?"

Rebecca spoke softly. "The man who killed Kristen. The man who is in my nightmares. The man who is stalking me."

Victoria finally realized that this was the secret Rebecca was keeping from Jared and her. *So, Rebecca did know something about Kristen's killer.* The girls helped Jared get Tony's body off of him and ran down the hall to find some help. If the killer was still in the mansion, they needed to find someone to help them.

David decided to look for Rebecca. Leana and Fred decided to take a walk and try to find her, as well. Leana and Fred heard a noise of some sort. They thought they heard a shout from someone, so they started to run. Leana stopped because she heard a noise and when she turned to see where the noise was coming from, she saw Sarah stuck on the wall like some sick trophy. She was still alive but she could barley breath. Leana went to her and tried to get her down, but she couldn't.

Sarah tried to speak, but her voice would not come out. Leana didn't know what to do. Sarah's eyes grew wide as she saw the Shadow Man standing behind Leana with a machete in his hand. As he raised his hand into a striking position, Sarah tried with all her might to warn Leana, who was crying, frustrated by her inability to save Sarah.

Fred noticed that Leana was missing, so he ran all the way back down the hall and saw the Shadow Man standing behind Leana.

"Leana! No!"

Leana turned around, but it was too late. The Shadow Man plunged the machete at Leana's delicate skin with the evil bloodthirsty blade. She was in shock as the warm blood dripped to her bare leg, exposed by the slit of her dress. She tried to mumble something, but she could not. The Shadow Man drove the blade deeper in Leana's back. He shoved the machete upwards, and blood poured out of Leana's mouth, turning her scream into a bloody gurgle. Her eyes went blank and then she fell to the floor like an unwanted rag doll.

The Shadow Man unmercifully pulled out the machete from her back. "Now for you lover boy."

Fred was so angry - so furious. Shadow Man started to go after him, but wanted to wait for the right moment. He came at Fred with all of his force, but Fred dodged him and he fell over the banister of the stair well, slamming to the floor. Fred ran and looked down from above. The Shadow Man didn't move an inch.

Fred turned back and ran to Leana. He picked her up in his arms and cradled her. He kissed her on her forehead. *Why her? Why my Leana?* The Shadow Man moved his fingers, stood up and wandered to the other wing to hunt for more of his prey.

Julie and Jonathan sat in their bedrooms quietly. It was dark and practically everyone was gone, so they had no idea what was going on. Julie sat on the bed with Jonathan. He looked at her and smiled. "You know what we could do to pass some time. We could, you know."

She looked at him and smiled, nodding her head. He gave her a big juicy kiss, and Julie, on impulse, pushed him on the bed and then sat on top of him, facing him. She began to unbuckle his pants. As her hands trailed down to his zipper, he laughed a little but then began to undo the buttons on her top.

He took off his shirt revealing his muscular body. Julie smiled and kissed him. Their lips locked.

Cathy and Jeremy were in Rebecca's room now. They couldn't find the cell phone anywhere, so Jeremy decided to go to Julie and Jonathan's room because he had a hunch that they had the phone with them.

The Shadow Man walked across the hallway, but stopped in his tracks when he saw the sidewall. There hung two long hunting spears. He walked up to the wall and pulled off one of the spears. He heard giggling coming from Julie and Jonathan's bedroom, and he could see Julie all over Jonathan. He walked into the bedroom slowly.

Rebecca didn't know where she was going, but she suddenly bumped into David. "Oh thank God. Tony is dead and I can't find the others."

Rebecca shut her eyes. *Why is this happening to me? That's it. As soon as I can, I will talk to someone so I can finally figure out what is going on? And then maybe I can find out what this killer has to do with my nightmares, also what he really wants and why he is tormenting all of us. But that can only happen if I survive this night.*

So much for a peaceful weekend. Life sucks. David suddenly realized something. "Rebecca, where's your cell phone?" She stared blankly at him for a second, but then remembered what she had done with it. "Julie wanted to borrow it. I haven't seen her. Do you think that she could be..." David grabbed Rebecca and gave her a big squeeze. He was also scared. "Let's give her a call okay?" Rebecca nodded her head.

David began to dial Rebecca's phone number, and it began to ring. After a few rings, a voice answered the phone. "Hello, Julie is that you?" The voice on the other line was quiet - it did not belong to Julie. Then the line went dead. David looked at Rebecca. "The phone went dead."

A grief stricken Fred found the worried gang. His tears looked dried up but his face looked as if it was consumed with anger. He walked over to Rebecca and David and almost choked out the words. "Leana is dead. I saw her get killed."

Rebecca started to get worried. *Oh my God. What if? No! No!* Rebecca got even more upset when Fred told the news that Leana was dead. *That poor girl* thought Rebecca. Then, suddenly, she went into a daze and fell to the floor. David and the others were shocked when she started to mumble. David checked her vitals and realized that Rebecca hadn't fainted; she had gone to sleep. She stood up by herself and started to walk upstairs.

"What the hell? What is she doing"

Victoria, who was a psychology major, gave everyone the answer they were asking. "I don't know what is going on but she seems to be sleepwalking again. Maybe she will lead us to Julie. She seems to sleep walk into a lot of danger. That must be it. If we are going to find anyone else we have to follow her."

Everyone agreed. Victoria telephoned the police. David and Fred decided to follow Rebecca, and the others decided to go outside and wait for the police to arrive. Fred and David slowly followed

Rebecca up the stairs. They had to make sure that she didn't get attacked while she was sleep walking.

Rebecca's mind began to see strange images. She saw Cathy, Jeremy, Jonathan and Julie. *That means that the killer must be after them, I must go and help them.* Rebecca began to turn down the left hall.

Julie was in bliss. *Jonathan is so fine.* Their kisses began to last longer. Julie pushed Jonathan down on top of the bed and said to him in a soft and sexy voice that she was going to rock his world. Jonathan closed his eyes and waited for the pleasure to begin. The Shadow Man rose behind Julie with the spear aimed to kill Julie and Jonathan at the same time.

The Shadow Man was going to plunge the spear right through Julie and into Jonathan. *Since they don't seem to want to separate, they can both be stuck together.* Jonathan moaned with pleasure, but then opened his eyes to see a dark figure behind Julie.

Cathy and Jeremy were about a few doors away from Julie and Jonathan's bedroom. They were tired because they had been running for so long. Jonathan just stared in terror at the dark figure that stood behind Julie. The figure finally took a step forward and Jonathan got a better look at him. His eyes grew wide with fear.

The Shadow Man plunged the spear into Julie's direction. Jonathan quickly rolled himself and Julie off the bed, just in time, as the spear rammed right into the bed. Julie looked up and saw the Shadow Man. She screamed and got up to run, but the Shadow Man cut her ankle with a knife that he had hidden underneath his coat. Jeremy and Cathy heard screams and came running into the room, to see the Shadow Man standing in front of Julie and Jonathan.

Cathy looked around and spotted a fire extinguisher. She broke the glass casing that it was in and then ran back into the room and sprayed it at the Shadow Man. Jonathan grabbed Julie and then the two of them escaped from the room. All four ran down the hallway but were stopped by a dead end. Jeremy looked around and saw a window.

The only way out was to climb the roof and then walk over to the other side where they could easily jump into the pool. The Shadow Man came into their view, standing in the middle of the hallway with a meat clever in his hand. He was not going to let them go alive.

Rebecca had a feeling that there was somebody following her, so she slipped out of view. David and Fred lost view of where she had gone. It was them that Rebecca had a feeling of, but she thought it was the killer.

Rebecca walked until she was standing right behind the Shadow Man, holding the other spear from the same wall the Shadow Man had found his. Rebecca decided to take Madame Mystique's advice about defeating nightmares, so she decided that she had had enough of the Shadow Man. Just as he was going to strike her friends, Rebecca came running down the hall. The spear plunged right through the Shadow Man's body.

Rebecca kept running, unable to stop. Her strength moved the Shadow Man forward until she gave the spear one final push and launched him right through the window. He crashed against the glass and then fell to the ground. David caught her before she could run out the window as well.

David shook Rebecca until she finally woke up. Everyone gave her a big hug. *What is going on?* Rebecca had no idea what had just happened. The police arrived and everyone was safely out of the mansion.

The policeman went over to David and told him that the killer was dead and that it was Bobby, Rebecca's driving instructor. Adam had the police check out his apartment and they found hundreds of pictures of Rebecca and her friends, so there was proof that he had been stalking Rebecca and the others.

The Shadow Man watched everyone leave. *I will get you Rebecca. I will kill you Tanya.* The Shadow Man pulled out the spear and cried out in agony. Luckily the spear did not puncture anything serious. *Her strength, her courage to face me. That wasn't Rebecca's. It was Tanya's. Time to turn Rebecca back into the girl she was once before. Time to make her Tanya once again.*

This time I will kill her for good. Any chance I get. He left the grounds and disappeared. Madame Mystique sat on the bus with all the others who had not been killed that night. She had slipped and hit her head, but she heard what had happened. Rebecca just stared out the window. *The killer is dead. I can move on.* But then she had a vision which made her change her mind.

In her vision she saw the Shadow Man once again. Even though she had not seen the Shadow Man, she knew that he must have been the killer. She knew that this fight was not over. She knew that she would someday have to face the terror by herself - one day.

CHAPTER 6

Two weeks had passed since the terrible slayings of Leana, Sarah and Tony, but Rebecca could not forget the horrible events that took place. She was so frightened about what had happened that she would wake up screaming in the middle of the night. Cathy and Julie understood how she felt, having witnessed the horror as well. No one remained the same after that weekend.

David, Jonathan and Jeremy apologized to Rebecca for not believing in her. Jonathan also secretly apologized to Cathy for not believing her either. Victoria and Jared were upset that Rebecca had kept a secret from them, but then they also understood that she was not even sure if what she had suspected was true or not.

Rebecca still felt that the terror was not over. No, she felt that it had just begun. School was out for a week due to a lengthy board meeting. December had finally arrived, and it had snowed a few days ago, but now there was no snow visible. However, the winter chill still blew through the air.

Rebecca was looking forward to meeting Madame Mystique. She thought that the psychic could actually help her unlock all the mysterious questions that she needed answered - she certainly couldn't answer them herself.

Cathy had arranged for Rebecca to have a revitalizing day. She scheduled a massage and hair appointment for her. Rebecca walked silently to the hair salon. *I guess my hair does need to be colored again. I don't like it when it turns too blond.*

She was lost in a stream of different thoughts. She now felt different and she had even started to act different. Something else also bothered her - she had not seen Keith around in many weeks. *I wonder where he is. It does not matter to me.* She pushed open the door to the salon and walked in.

Sofia, the red headed beautician, smiled as Rebecca took a seat, and told her that she would be just a minute. The girl was one of her friends from school. Sofia told Rebecca that she would be a minute, even though here were hardly any customers in the salon. The last customer had paid and then left, leaving Rebecca and Sofia alone in the salon.

"Hello Beck. So what can I do you for today?"

Rebecca laughed, amused by Sofia's country accent. "Well, the usual and maybe even a trim. Cathy is paying for it, after all."

Sofia smiled and told her to sit in a chair. "Okay then. Let me just mix the hair color and then I will be right with you as soon as I can. Okay."

Sofia left the room and went into the back room where she kept all the chemicals. She came back after a little while carrying a squeeze bottle with hair color. She slowly put the hair color in Rebecca's hair and then wrapped a towel around her head. Rebecca was then told to stay put for about an hour. Sofia remembered that she needed to go to the bank to withdraw some money to pay her rent.

"I have to go to the bank, so I need you to do me a favor."

"Fine. I know the drill. I will assist the customers until you come back. Right?"

Sofia nodded her head and then grabbed her jacket and left. Rebecca sat all alone by herself. Her eyes started to shut. She felt tired. Rebecca was secretly keeping herself awake, afraid that she would see visions of what had happened at Victoria's again.

But she finally had to surrender to the sleep and her body felt like it was floating. She ended up in a hallway leading to a room. She caught her reflection in the mirror. *Not again!* Rebecca was wearing a beautiful gown and her hair was tied up in a bun. There were voices coming from within the room, so she hesitantly walked up to the door, opened it and walked into the room.

At that instant she was swept into a large dancing hall where everyone was wearing a party dress and laughing, smiling, and shouting. It seemed that she had entered a gala, or a party. Despite the revelry, she remained very tense, afraid that the Shadow Man would appear and attack her. But he did not come.

Maybe he has finally left me alone. He must have been a figment of my imagination. Rebecca relaxed a bit and began to enjoy the party. She walked over and sat with a bunch of Tanya's old friends. Across from her sat Claudia Carmel, who was Tanya's best friend in the whole world. Amy Winchester, another good friend, sat beside Claudia. Three other men and a girl also were at the table.

Rebecca recognized them from the picture she had seen in one of her dreams. The man sitting beside her was Steven Lancaster and the man sitting on the other side of her was Daniel Peters. The other man was Jack - Tanya's Jack. The girl who was sitting beside him was Samantha Peters. *Everyone's here but Isabella. I wonder where she is.*

"Where is Isabella? I thought that she would have come to this ball. It is not like her to miss such a glorious event, you know."

Jack looked at Rebecca and answered her question. "Isabella is ill and at home. She is upset that she could not make it. Poor girl. It is not that same without her here with us."

Steven heard his favorite song play and asked Rebecca to dance with him. The others also rose and partnered up. Rebecca smiled, feeling quite enchanted. *Now this is the type of dream I want. Relaxing and fantastic. Even though this is Tanya's time I feel like I belong here with all of them.* Rebecca looked over at Jack. *Especially him.*

A sudden noise of glass breaking made Rebecca wake up. She sat up in her chair and looked all around the shop. Her breathing had been so relaxed, but now her pulse quickened.

Rebecca heard another noise.

"Who's there?"

Rebecca turned around to see if there was anyone else beside herself in the salon, but there was only silence. She was sure that she had heard a noise. *Strange. Maybe I am just getting paranoid.* She headed back to the front of the salon.

"What could be taking Sofia so long? I wonder if she has any magazines in the back room."

Rebecca was about to go to the back room when she suddenly caught a glimpse of herself in the mirror. "My hair. Oh my God, my hair! The color, it isn't mine! Its... it's a totally different color!" Rebecca ran to the sink and began to rinse her hair. After rinsing her hair she then dried it. Rebecca now stood in front of the large full sized mirror. There in front of her stood a carbon copy of Tanya Annabella Arkenson - the girl from her dreams, and her nightmares.

"What's going on? Why? It can't be. That can't be me. That's her, not me. What's happening to me?"

Rebecca began to cry. She was so infuriated that she slammed her fist against the mirror, shattering it. The shards of the mirror spread all over the floor. The soft, ivory skin on her hand began to be enveloped by dark red. Her blood was scattered amongst all the broken pieces of the mirror. When she realized what she had done, she hurriedly ran to the back room to get the first aid kit.

When she found it, she took out a bottle of alcohol and began to rub it gently on her knuckles that she had cut. Her screams echoed throughout the salon, and tears streaked down her face. Her green eyes glistened in the rays of sunlight that crept in through the windows. A feeling of nausea spread all over her body - she was so weak and tired.

Rebecca knew what she was feeling, and she also knew that this time she could not possible hold it back. She began to feel the excruciating pain in her stomach and head worse than it ever was before. Her knees began to wobble, her eyes began to twitch and her body felt numb. She fell to the floor as her mind began to register strange and terrifying images. Her vision began to blur and she saw a frightening image of a man wearing a black overcoat, holding a large butcher knife. He was running after a familiar looking girl. Rebecca tried to concentrate and figure out who the young girl was. She was trying to see if she could see her face but a sudden noise in the salon made Rebecca come out of her psychic trance.

"Who's there?"

Rebecca was getting sick and tired of this game of cat and mouse, so she headed back to the front of the salon. There was no one in sight, but when she turned around she saw a message written on the wall. "Tanya, you always looked better with your natural hair color. Ain't that right… Rebecca?"

She began to back away from the wall, frightened beyond belief by what she had read. She ran to the front door and was lucky enough to slip before the silent figure hiding behind the door slashed a knife at her.

"So we meet again, Tanya. I think it's about time you had a cut."

Rebecca looked up at the man and saw that he was the same man from her vision. In his hand he clutched a sharp looking butcher knife that gleamed like sinful evil. She tried to get up and run, but her fall had sprained her ankle, and she was trapped.

"Now stay still. I'll make sure that I don't cut you too deep. I promise."

Rebecca could not believe her eyes. *He's real. He's really real. The man from my dreams. The man who I saw kill Tanya. He's real and he's still alive. That bastard killed an innocent girl and everyone thought that she had committed suicide. Wait. This man. He is the same guy who murdered Kristen. The guy who was at Victoria's mansion.*

"Any final words?"

Rebecca gripped the lead pipe that was on the floor beside her. She looked up to him and said in a ticked off voice, "Eat lead you son of a bitch."

Rebecca slammed the lead pipe into his hand, and the knife fell to the floor. Then she hit him on his knees, stood up and slammed his face with the pipe. She managed to get by him and then she started to run. *I have to get out of here. He didn't kill all those people because he was some crazed murderer; he killed them because of me. Maybe he knows that I know the truth of what really happened to Tanya. I have to get help.* Rebecca looked over her shoulder and she saw the Shadow Man striding towards her. He was pissed off. His hand gripped a pair of sharp sheers. *Oh no.*

Rebecca ran down the steps leading to the subway station. She limped with pain as her ankle bones began to make creaking sounds. There was a trail of blood behind her as she ran to the subway. When she turned back, she saw the Shadow Man right behind her, taking his time. She screamed and ran into the subway train, just as the doors locked.

Rebecca had tears running down her cheek. She didn't know what to do. The man from her nightmares was actually the man who was in her reality and now he wanted her dead. Unlike a dream, she knew that it was going to be impossible to get away from him so easily.

Rebecca turned her head to see a familiar face in the next train. Rebecca stood up and limped with all her might to the door leading to the other train. Lana sat in the seat in the next train reading a magazine. Rebecca banged on the door, trying to get her attention. Lana yawned and then looked up. She saw Rebecca and smiled.

"Hey. What are you doing here?"

Rebecca tried to speak but Lana could not hear her. Lana made a confused face telling Rebecca that she could not hear her. Lana was now against her door looking at Rebecca. Rebecca turned around to see who else was in the train with her. A gang of guys sat on the other side that might have been Spanish or even Italian. The guys were eyeing Rebecca and they were staring at her.

They began to whistle and holler. "Hey baby, why don't you come and sit over here with us. We won't bite, unless you want us to."

They started to laugh. *Male slime* thought Rebecca. She turned back around to face Lana, who was alone on the train. Out of the corner of her eye, Rebecca spotted movement at the end of Lana's train. A dark figure mustered about behind the seats.

Rebecca strained her eyes. Lana noticed Rebecca staring towards the back, so she slowly turned her head, but she did not see anything. Lana turned around to face Rebecca, who continued staring. Finally, the figure rose up from the seat, and the Shadow Man emerged. He had his weapon in his hand, aimed and ready for the target.

Rebecca screamed. The guys in the train stopped doing what they were doing and stared at her. "Hey sweetie, what ya screaming for?"

She slammed her fists against the door, continuing to scream. Lana could tell she was screaming and that she was upset. "Rebecca, why are you screaming? What is it? What?"

Lana noticed that Rebecca was pointing to something behind her, so she around and saw the Shadow Man. She yelped and then began to scream, banging against the window. Rebecca became hysterical as the Shadow Man caught up to Lana. His hand gripped her throat, and he raised her a few feet off the ground.

His hand gripped the sheers. Rebecca saw the emergency stop breaks on the side of the train and darted to the switch. The Shadow Man let go of Lana, who hit the floor but managed to scurry towards the door. Rebecca pushed the buttons for the break and the subway trains all began to shake as the emergency breaks kicked in.

The Shadow Man lost his balance and fell. Lana was flung into the side of the train. Rebecca fell and hit her head. The gang of guys fell out of their seats and started to yell and complain. The train came to a complete stop. Lana got up and grabbed the sheers that fell from the Shadow Man's hand and stood up with shaking hands. She had never felt this type of fear before.

Rebecca had to get out of the subway train and help her. She ran back to where the guys sat, took their boom box and rammed it into the door until it broke. She threw the boom box aside and opened the door. She unlocked the door leading into Lana's train, where the Shadow Man lay on the floor.

Rebecca assured Lana that everything would be all right as she crept over the Shadow Man. She watched him carefully. Her foot rested near his hand. Lana walked cautiously towards Rebecca. Her foot trembled but she managed to walk over the Shadow Man and run into the next train.

Rebecca turned around in relief. The gang of guys rushed over. Some were pissed and some were curious about what was going on. Lana told them about the attempted attack. Rebecca was now staring at the guys. She did not see the Shadow Man's hand move, or twitch, but her ankle felt like it was swelling.

The Shadow Man's hand spread out and grabbed Rebecca's broken ankle and she yelped in pain. He squeezed her ankle so tight that everyone else on the train could hear the bones crack. She fell to the floor. Lana yelled and ran over to her and plunged the sheers into the Shadow Man's arm.

He let go and growled. Lana helped Rebecca up and then the two ran behind all the guys. They grabbed their chains and knives and stood around the Shadow Man. "You screwed up freak. Chasing after a girl. We are going to teach you a lesson."

The Shadow Man smiled an evil smile. He stood up and waited for them to attack him. The first guy whipped his chain at him, but the Shadow Man caught it with his right hand and grabbed the guy by his neck. The Shadow Man broke the guy's neck. Everyone heard a loud crack and the boy's body went limp. He threw the body to the ground and waited for the next attack.

Rebecca grabbed one of the guy's baseball bat. She started to slam it against the glass. The glass was too hard to break but she managed to crack it. The next guy took out his knife and slashed at the Shadow Man. The guy maneuvered himself and finally he stabbed him in the ribs. The guy smiled, but the Shadow Man pulled out a hidden weapon and stuck it into the guy's spine.

He then raised him and dropped him to the floor. He pulled out a knife and then with out any hesitation grabbed the last two guys' by their throats and with one yank he twisted both of their necks. Lana turned and saw all the guys dead on the floor.

"Hurry, up Rebecca. He's coming. He's coming."

Rebecca saw the Shadow Man walking towards them. She raised the bat up high and with all the might that she had left smashed the window open. Rebecca threw the bat at the Shadow Man and then the two girls crawled out of the window and ran towards the emergency staircase.

Rebecca limped as fast as she could regardless of the horrible pain in her ankle. *He must have broken more bones.* Rebecca and Lana finally reached the emergency exit. They opened the door and ran upstairs. Lana could not believe it. There was a man really stalking Rebecca.

"Rebecca, are you okay?"

Rebecca yelped in pain from her hurt ankle. She gave Lana the phone and told her to call for help. She called David but no one was home, so she called Victoria. Victoria told them not to move from where they were and went to find Jared.

Rebecca's vision started to blur and sweat began to drip down her head. She was burning up. Lana shook her, but she began to faint. "No, no you can't faint." Rebecca fainted. Lana pulled her to a dark corner near a house. She had no choice; she needed to find help.

She walked to one of the houses where the lights were on and knocked on the door. A man answered the door. Lana was surprised to see that the man standing in the doorway was Mr. Hiller. "Mr. Hiller. I didn't know you lived here." He was surprised to see Lana, one of his students, at his door. "I have been here for about three years now, Lana. What are you doing here?"

She told him about the attempted attack, and he telephoned the police and then picked Rebecca up into his arms and placed her on the couch. He got some medicine and some ice and his first aid kit to wrap her ankle up.

Lana was so relieved to find Mr. Hiller. *Thank God. Now we are safe.* Rebecca began to mumble to herself. Lana was covered with drops of blood. The police said that they would be there soon, so Lana excused herself and went to wash her face.

When she came back downstairs she found an unconcious Mr. Hiller. The door was wide open and Rebecca was not on the couch. Her muscles began to tense with fear. She heard a noise. She looked to her right and saw Rebecca walking towards the basement door.

Lana slowly followed her as she walked towards the basement door. Lana turned back to see if Mr. Hiller was still alive. He had a pulse and was breathing. Lana grabbed a walking stick that she found nearby.

She walked down the stairs, but she could not see Rebecca. When she felt a cold draft come upon her, she stopped and turned back to look up the stairs. There stood the Shadow Man, with a hammer in his hand. Lana screamed and quickly went in search of Rebecca.

Lana ran from room to room. There was only one room left but she ran right into the Shadow Man. Lana stood still. The walking stick dropped from her hand. The Shadow Man caressed her cheek and she began to cry.

He raised the hammer up high. Lana started to choke on her cries. The Shadow Man spoke. "I am not going to let you interfere with my plans. I am going to kill your friend Rebecca. She does not deserve to live just like Tanya didn't deserve to live."

Lana's eyes widened. *Did he just say Tanya? That's the girl Rebecca keeps on dreaming about. Oh my God. This man must be the guy who killed Tanya. That makes sense. For some odd reason, Rebecca is having visions about Tanya's murder. Rebecca knows that Tanya was not a suicide victim. Rebecca knows that Tanya was murdered and this man...this man must be the same man who killed Tanya.*

Before the Shadow Man could say anything more the door to the last room suddenly swung open and Rebecca stood in the doorway. The Shadow Man just stood there and watched her, as well as Lana. Suddenly, all the bulbs in the basement began to flicker on and off.

The basement began to shake, and the windows broke. The Shadow Man's hammer flew out of his hand and into the wall. Rebecca's eyes opened and then the Shadow Man was slammed into the wall by an unseen force. He got up and ran back up the stairs.

The wind stopped and then Rebecca fell to the floor. Lana stood paralyzed for a few moments. *What just happened?* Lana came out of her bewildered thoughts when the police arrived, along with Victoria and Jared.

Lana told Victoria everything that had happened. Jared got worried. The Shadow Man was not dead after all and now there was proof that there was a Tanya. The only person that could help Rebecca and the rest of them was Madame Mystique. But none of them would see her until the carnival.

I hope my aunt can find out what is going on, she was always able to find anything out. I hope she can, for my sake, the others sake, and Rebecca's sake. But, they couldn't find anything out until the carnival. Mr. Hiller was taken to the hospital. His knock on the head was pretty hard.

Lana started to cry but then she stopped. Rebecca had finally awakened. Lana hugged her friend. Rebecca was happy to see Victoria and Jared. But for some strange reason, Rebecca felt different; powerful. *Who knows* thought Rebecca. *Maybe I have a new attitude.*

CHAPTER 7

Rebecca awoke from her sleep. She had been sleeping quite a bit since the last attack, but she had not had a nightmare in about two weeks. It was a miracle. She felt stronger and different. It was like everything went back to normal. David and the others were still trying to get used to Rebecca's new hair color. David had to admit now that she looked like the girl in the article that she had for her I.S.U., but that didn't mean that Rebecca had anything to do with that girl.

As for the Shadow Man, well David thought that he was just some crazed lunatic. So now it was confirmed that Rebecca had a stalker. Mr. Hiller stayed in the hospital for about three days, or so. Jonathan substituted for the class, and that made Julie happy. Everyone thought that Rebecca seemed very different; more distracted somehow.

Lana was trying to avoid being around Rebecca, still trying to figure out what happened at Mr. Hiller's house. She was still amazed at how the Shadow Man was suddenly flung into the wall. She was scared to go anywhere by herself so she decided to stay with Victoria.

Victoria and Jared hired an investigator to look into the matter. Adam had suggested Detective Michaels to Victoria. Detective Michaels was not convinced that the killer was actually stalking Rebecca. He believed that the man just hated college students.

David arrived at Rebecca's dorm. Julie, Cathy and Rebecca were already dressed. David walked into the dorm looking tense. He sat down on Rebecca's bed and she noticed worry on his face.

"David, what's wrong?"

David looked at Rebecca and then he looked at Cathy and Julie.

"Girls, we have a problem. My brother, my older brother Damian is coming for a visit. He is a pain."

Cathy rolled her eyes and Julie started to laugh. Rebecca though didn't. Julie and Cathy both had siblings. Rebecca didn't have any brothers, or sisters. She really wished that she did though. That way she would have someone to talk to. She sometimes wished that she had some family in town but all her family lived in other countries and she didn't know them very well.

"David, I think it's nice that your brother is coming for a visit. I mean, I would love to have a brother, or even a sister."

David smiled a little and then looked at Rebecca, who stood completely still. Her mind ached and her eyes hurt. Her balance started getting bad. She felt sharp pains in her stomach, and fell to the floor in pain. David and the others ran to Rebecca.

"Becky, what's wrong?"

Rebecca could not reply. So many visions came flashing in her mind once again. She saw poor Tanya cry in agony before she was thrown from her window once again. She then saw Kristen being thrown out of the window. Rebecca saw Jack crying near a grave.

Suddenly, all the visions stopped and she felt perfectly fine. Rebecca stood up. David didn't say anything. Neither did Cathy and the others. Rebecca sat on the bed, closed her eyes and then opened them again.

David walked over to her and asked once again if she was all right and what had happened. "David, Cathy, Julie. It was happening again. I started seeing things again. Visions. Visions of that girl's murder. Tanya. I don't know what's happening to me. I think I might be going crazy."

Rebecca started to cry. David began to comfort her. Cathy and Julie looked at each other. Everything she had been saying sounded weird but they both had seen the Shadow Man. They also knew that Rebecca had strange feelings whenever something strange or bad was going to happen. They knew that there was some truth to what she was saying.

As for Tanya, Lana had confirmed that. She told everyone that the Shadow Man had mentioned her name. "Rebecca, you're not crazy." A voice came from someone else in the room. David looked to see Victoria with Jared.

"Victoria, what are you doing here?" Victoria was shocked at Rebecca's sudden attitude change. Her voice sounded almost mean.

"Rebecca, I came to see if you were feeling better. I think I know who can help you."

Rebecca wiped her tears away. "Who?" Victoria was almost scared to suggest her aunt but it was worth a try. "My aunt. She's going to be at the carnival today. You did want to go see her, didn't you?"

Rebecca had completely forgotten about Madame Mystique. *I bet she could shed some light on this whole thing with the Shadow Man. But I'll be there with everyone, can I really chance it?* David smiled at Victoria and winked at Cathy and Julie. They got what point he was trying to get across.

"Rebecca, it'll be good for you to get out and, plus, that way my brother can meet everyone. So, what do you say?" Rebecca knew that she could not argue with David so she nodded her head. Everyone got up and left the room. Rebecca changed her clothes and met everyone outside. *I hope that all my questions will be answered. I hope.*

The carnival was bigger than the last time. There were more booths and rides. Rebecca smiled. She hadn't smiled for a long time. The atmosphere of the carnival made her feel like a little girl again and she was full of joy at watching other little girl's laughing and also crying on the rides.

She remembered that her father had forced her to go on a roller coaster. She was terrified of those things but ever since that day, she loved them. David's brother was going to meet everyone later on at the carnival.

Fred joined the rest of them. Lana didn't want to come but she did anyway. Rebecca was having a lot of fun. She turned her eyes towards David. "David, I am so glad we all decided to come here. I feel happy, thank you."

David was so happy to hear that. He gave her a warm kiss. Victoria started to giggle. Rebecca stopped kissing David and then made a funny comment. "Why are we laughing?" Victoria stopped laughing but then started to laugh louder. "I'm laughing because when David kisses you it looks like a giant vacuum trying to suck dust. That means your the dust."

Rebecca made a face. "Oh, that does it. You're the one that's going to be dust, missy. Come here you." Rebecca laughed and ran after Victoria. Julie and Cathy started to laugh.

About an hour later they all arrived at Madame Mystique's booth. Lana, Fred, Jonathan and Jared decided not to join the rest of them because they still wanted to look around. Julie, Cathy, David, Jeremy and Victoria were there though. Rebecca was thankful, but also a little nervous. She had no idea what she was going to find out.

Everyone walked inside and the smell of vanilla, sage and sandalwood incense took over. There were beads hanging from the ceiling. It looked like somewhere a gypsy might live. Cathy thought it was creepy. Julie thought it was interesting. David just thought it was pathetic.

"I knew you would come Rebecca."

There in front of them stood Madame Mystique, wearing an elegant scarf. She looked powerful. In front of her was a table with lit candles and a deck of tarot cards on it.

She hugged Victoria and greeted everyone else. She then motioned everyone else to take a seat around the table. Madame Mystique sat across from Rebecca. Rebecca breathed in and let out a sigh - a sigh that was a little too loud. Cathy and Julie began to laugh.

Madame Mystique began to speak in soft and reassuring tones. "Dear, now tell me what's troubling you? You look confused and full of questions. I want to help you as much as I can."

Rebecca started to cry a little but she then managed to get control of her emotions. "Madame Mystique, I want to know why I keep having these strange visions. Also, I want to know why I am being stalked. I want to know why the man from my nightmares is actually alive and in my reality."

Madame Mystique nodded her head. "Okay. Okay dear. I know what we can do. I know who we can get all these answers from."

Rebecca's face lit up. "Really? You know somebody that can give me answers. Who?" Everyone else was taken by the conversations that all their faces were full of curiosity. They were waiting for an answer from Madame Mystique.

"Well, the person is close to you Rebecca. You know her very well. In fact she lives with you."

Madame Mystique then stared at Cathy, who looked bewildered. But then Madame Mystique looked at Julie and the others as well. "Rebecca, who do you know that you are very close to?"

Rebecca thought for herself. *I have no idea.* "I don't know."

Madame Mystique then got up and said the answer in a slow voice. "That person is yourself Rebecca. You have all the answers."

Me. Rebecca got up in confusion. *Some psychic you are. Honestly.* But then she wondered what Madame Mystique was getting at. "Me. So how can I find out the answers?"

Victoria made a face. *Oh no. No. No. Not a regression.* "A regression. I am going to hypnotize you and take you to your past life."

Rebecca started to laugh. David also giggled. Madame Mystique knew that Rebecca believed her but was trying to avoid the truth. "If your past has not been resolved, then it shall affect your present and it may even destroy your future…"

Everyone stopped laughing. Her words were so serious. Rebecca gulped. *Maybe what she is saying is true, but I don't know.* Madame Mystique was not going to argue because she knew that Rebecca would come to her when she wanted to.

"I know you are trying to help me but I don't know if I believe what you are trying to indicate. I am sorry."

Madame Mystique nodded her head in agreement. Everyone got up and left. But before Victoria left Madame Mystique gave her a letter. Victoria put the letter in her pocket.

Rebecca remained quiet the whole evening. Madame's words were still echoing through her mind. David met Fred, Lana and Jonathan. Jared went to get David's brother. David was not looking forward to meeting his brother.

David's brother was twenty-three, and was the better looking one in the family. He was taller than David, more muscled and he was the son that his parents loved and adored the most. Damian was his name and making his little brother's life miserable was his job. He often tried to take David's girlfriends away and often he managed to do it. But this time David was with Rebecca and there was no way that he was going to give her up without a fight.

Jared arrived with Damian. Damian was wearing tears offs and a black shirt. As usual he looked good. Cathy stared at Damian, as did Julie, Victoria and Lana. Their eyes were filled with shock. Damian was so handsome.

He was tall with black hair. He had dimples, and a goatee. His eyes had the coolest mix between green and brown. Julie smiled a little but then Jonathan glared at her. Jeremy did the same to Cathy and Jared did the same to Victoria. The girls' cooled down and looked away. Lana kept on staring until Fred purposely nudged into her.

Rebecca turned and saw Damian. To Rebecca he was just

another good looking guy on legs. Nothing else. Rebecca went over to David. "Is that your brother? He does not look like you at all." David was so relieved. Damian stared at Rebecca, looking her up from head to toe. She was wearing a pair of blue jeans and a pink sweater.

He was impressed by his brother's choice. Damian smiled at all the other girls. He went over to David and gave his brother a big bear hug. He then introduced himself to everyone else and they smiled and introduced themselves.

The carnival was going to close in about four more hours, so everyone decided to split up and meet later. Rebecca was with David and Damian. Julie went with Jonathan to the log ride. Cathy and Jeremy went to the fun house. Lana and Fred went on the go-carts cars. Victoria and Jared went to the ferris wheel.

Rebecca saw the antique carousel. The tune made her stare at the ride with fascination. When she was little, this was her favorite. It still was. She got in line and waited for her turn. David decided to let Rebecca go on it alone.

Rebecca sat on a white horse. As the carousal turned and turned, she began to have a strange feeling that she had been on the same carousel before. She suddenly had a vision of Tanya, laughing and smiling. *This is the first time that I have ever seen her smile.* Rebecca blinked and realized that she had drifted into another Tanya thought. *Don't think about her.*

As Rebecca spun around and around she did not see, or notice, a dark figure watching her. The Shadow Man hid in the shadows watching her, with a meat cleaver in his hand. *I am going to have a lot of fun today. I am going to get my point across to all of your friends.* The Shadow Man left to find someone, when he saw Julie and Jonathan standing in line for the log ride.

Julie fidgeted with her hair. *How much longer? I hate waiting in lines.* She rolled her eyes but then her eyes stopped at Jonathan. He looked great. He was wearing his shorts and a white see through shirt. She was happy to be with him. He was the only male figure in her life since her father died. She lived with her mother.

Julie's sisters and her brother did not live with them. They had places of their own. Julie missed them from time to time, but she always remained happy. Jonathan looked at her and noticed that she looked dazed. "Hey. Chicklet, move."

Julie smiled and shoved him a little. "Chicklet" was her nickname. Julie and Jonathan got into the log ride. Even before the ride began to move she started to scream. Jonathan started to laugh, thinking that she was so weird sometimes. He remembered once when she went on so many scary rides that she threw up in front of him. He was so shocked. He ran over to her to ask if she was all right, but she just walked over to the beanie baby stand and said, "They are so cute, don't you think?"

Jonathan was so shocked. He now looked at Julie remembering that day. Julie saw him staring at her, and knew what he was thinking. "Jonathan, are you still thinking of that day I threw up and walked over to the toy stand acting like nothing happened? Because if you are, get over it."

Jonathan started to laugh, and Julie smiled. She had her arms wrapped around his waist. The log went up the long hill and entered the dark cave. They finally turned the corner in the cave and were close to the drop.

Julie started to scream and Jonathan decided *what the hell* and he also started to yell and shout. The log began to shake. Both of them stopped screaming. They both knew the log was supposed to shake but it felt as if someone else was in it besides them. Julie turned her head back to see a menacing figure.

The Shadow Man stood in the back seat with the meat clever in his hand. Julie started to scream louder. Jonathan looked back and also started to yell. They were trapped. The Shadow Man struck at

Jonathan, but missed when Jonathan slipped and fell. Julie took out her can of pepper spray.

She held it up and said, "I think we have been through this before. Eat pepper you... you...you psycho." Julie sprayed the Shadow Man, and he could not believe that she had the nerve to spray him again. He was blinded, and he began to thrash the meat clever around. He managed to cut Julie's arm, and she screamed and she lost her balance.

Julie fell over the side of the log and ended up getting swept to the drop. Jonathan jumped in after her. The Shadow Man washed out his eyes with the water, feeling very angry. The Shadow Man jumped out of the log as well, and headed back towards the cave.

Julie's arm hurt and she could not even try to swim because of the pain. "Help me Jonathan. Help me!" Jonathan grabbed hold of her hand before she went over the drop and grabbed the railing. Julie dangled off the ledge of the drop as the log came towards them.

He pulled her out of the way just as the log came over the drop. Julie started to cry. They quickly found the emergency staircase and went to go warn all the others that the Shadow Man was at the carnival.

Cathy and Jeremy were walking around and around in the mirror maze. They were still stuck. Jeremy kept on bumping into the mirrors. Cathy was getting hungry, and she got upset, sat down in a corner and told Jeremy to find his way out so he could get some food. She was starving.

Jeremy reluctantly left and this time he actually found his way out. Cathy wondered why Madame Mystique was staring at her. *Spooky* thought Cathy. Cathy stood up and looked at herself in the mirror. She admired her beauty. *Gosh, I am so beautiful. I am a snob, after all.*

Cathy laughed to herself but stopped when she heard footsteps. Cathy kept quiet, noticing that the footsteps did not sound like

Jeremy's. Then the footsteps stopped. Cathy remained quiet. She turned and bumped into Jeremy, relieved that it was him. She flirtatiously hit him, and he grabbed her and gave her a kiss.

Cathy pushed him away and then attacked the food. She was tearing the chicken off the bone as if she had not eaten a thing in days. Jeremy, then and there, lost his appetite. He felt sick after watching Cathy scarf down the chicken.

Cathy saw that Jeremy had not eaten his Burger. "Are you not going to eat that?" Jeremy said no. Cathy smiled. "Good." She picked up the burger and ate it as well. Jeremy just waved his head back and forth until he heard a a scrapping sound, followed by footsteps.

"Cathy, did you hear that noise?" Cathy stopped munching her burger. She also heard the sound. She dropped the burger and stood up. *Where is that sound coming from?* She looked all around until she faced Jeremy. She then let out a frightened yelp. Behind Jeremy stood the Shadow Man.

Jeremy stared at Cathy. Her expression was totally frightening him. Jeremy turned around but there was no one there. He then looked at her. "What's wrong?" She couldn't speak. The Shadow Man was going to play with his prey before he finally pulled the final curtains on them.

She urged Jeremy to get her out of the fun house. She suddenly stopped when she heard an echo of her name. She turned to face a mirror. Jeremy saw Cathy staring into the mirror.

"I know your beautiful and you know that too. Now come on."

Cathy heard her name again. *This can't be.* The image of Cathy was replaced with the image of the Shadow Man standing behind Jeremy again. *No!* Cathy whirled around again. Jeremy looked at her. *Nothing*. She then heard her name again coming from the mirror. But wait, her name was not coming from behind the mirror, and she took a step back.

"Jeremy, I think there's someone behind the mirror." Jeremy walked over to the mirror and placed his ear against the mirror. He could hear someone breathing. Cathy was getting scared so she backed up into another mirror. The breathing stopped. Jeremy lifted his ear and then turned around.

"Cathy, I think the person is gone now. You got scared for no reason at all."

She sighed a little in relief, but suddenly a meat clever came crashing through the mirror she was leaning against. She turned around and screamed as the Shadow Man came through the mirror. He grabbed her by the neck and flung her into one of the mirrors and rammed Jeremy into another mirror.

Cathy took of her high heel and struck the Shadow Man's hand, causing him to drop the meat cleaver. The Shadow Man turned to Cathy and walked slowly towards her. *Rebecca help me!*

Rebecca was eating her ice cream when suddenly, her head began to hurt. She dropped the cone and Damian rushed to her side. "Hey, are you okay?" She looked into his dark and mysterious eyes as they burned into her soul. She nodded dreamily and then remembered that she was David's girlfriend.

David went to find the others. Rebecca's eyes shut for a moment but then she opened them. She had a strange feeling that she had to go to the roller coaster. "Damian, let's go on the roller coaster."

He smiled and accompanied her to the roller coaster named, The Monster. Rebecca wondered how everyone one else was, but then her mind drifted to Cathy.

I wonder how she is right now. The Shadow Man tried to grab Cathy but Jeremy rammed into him, sending him flying into a pair of mirrors. Jeremy grabbed Cathy and they made their way out of the funhouse, to warn the others.

Fred and Lana were having fun riding in the go-carts. It was their favorite ride, and Fred had finally gotten over Leana's death.

Poor Leana thought Lana. Fred and Lana were in separate cars, and there was hardly anybody on the ride. Lana started to laugh when someone kept on racing along side Fred. But then her laugh became a gulp.

A dark shadow was sitting in the car that was racing beside Fred's go-cart. It was the Shadow Man. Lana yelled out to Fred, but it was too late. The Shadow Man somehow made his car faster and stronger. He rammed into Fred's car causing him to fall out. The Shadow Man backed his car and got ready to hit Fred.

He was dazed as the Shadow Man sped forward. He was about to hit Fred, but Lana blocked his path. She smashed her car into the Shadow Man's and managed to knock him out of the car. She backed away and then went forward. She hit him so hard that he fell out of the go-cart rink. When Fred and Lana went to see if the Shadow Man was still there, they saw that he had vanished.

"Let's go. We have to find Rebecca. He's after her."

Victoria and Jared sat cuddled against each other, high up on the ferris wheel. Victoria felt like she was on top of the world. She remembered the letter her aunt had given her. Victoria pulled away from Jared and took out the letter.

The letter read, "Dear Victoria. Please, look after that poor girl. Rebecca is in grave danger. Victoria, Rebecca is like me but stronger, and you know what I mean. Watch her and help her. From: Your Aunt."

Victoria was scared. Her aunt was serious. The guy stalking Rebecca was going to kill her. Victoria saw Jared's strange expression. "What's wrong Jared?" He stared at the seats that were two away from theirs. Victoria followed his gaze until she saw the Shadow Man.

"Oh my God. It's the Shadow Man. Oh no, Rebecca."

Victoria shook Jared. Jared didn't know what to do but from where they sat, they could see Rebecca standing near the roller coaster with Damian. Victoria looked down to see Julie, Jonathan, Cathy, Fred, Jeremy and Lana. She took out her lipstick and wrote a message. She then took off her shoe and threw it down at them. The shoe hit Cathy in the head and she winced in pain and looked up. It took her a while to spot Victoria.

"Hey, it's Victoria and Jared."

Julie squinted her eyes. "And the Shadow Man. Look." They all looked to see the Shadow Man trying to climb to Victoria and Jared's seat, and Cathy picked up the shoe because she saw a piece of paper.

Jeremy took the paper and read it out loud. "Guys, help, go warn Rebecca, she's at the roller coaster with Damian." Fred and Lana ran to the roller coaster to warn Rebecca but she was gone and so was Damian.

"We have got to help them." Julie was more concerned with Jared and Victoria's predicament. The Shadow Man reached the seat that the two were in, knocked Jared out of the car and he sat beside Victoria. He took out a piece of mirror.

"Prepare to die, Victoria Grace." Victoria began to scream. The Shadow Man launched his hand towards her but she grabbed on to it. Her hand began to bleed. *Help me. Wait. Rebecca was like my aunt. Maybe, just maybe. If she was like my aunt then she would help me.* In her mind Victoria cried out for help.

Rebecca's head began to hurt as she sat across Damian on the roller coaster. She heard Victoria's cries for help. Rebecca's eyes closed but then reopened, and a strong wind began to arise and blow towards the ferris wheel. The Shadow Man saw Rebecca's reflection from the piece of mirror that he held in his hand. *It can't be.* The image faded and then it became Tanya. Victoria saw that the Shadow Man was distracted, so she kicked him and pushed him hard, causing him to fall out of the seat, and land in a swimming pool near the others.

Victoria saw Rebecca standing near the roller coaster staring at her, but then she fainted. *Rebecca you did it. You saved me.* Julie got the ride operator to get Victoria and Jared down. The police arrived and went to the pool, but the Shadow Man had disappeared. David arrived at the scene and asked everyone what happened and showed them the strange letter he had received.

The letter said, "Whatever goes up, must come down." He laughed, but Victoria and the others started to run towards the roller coaster. David began running towards the roller coaster as well and saw Rebecca in Damian's arms. "Now what has he done? What the hell is going on?"

A noise of metal breaking made everyone stop in their tracks. Damian looked up to see the roller coaster's tracks bust and pieces of the track began to fall everywhere. A piece of track headed in David's direction, but he saw it and jumped out of the way.

Finally the roller coaster fell off the track. Screams echoed throughout the carnival. Julie and the others all ducked. Rebecca awoke and started to scream when she saw that the roller coaster had begun to descend towards the ground.

Damian couldn't move, as the roller coaster came towards him. Rebecca got up and ran towards him. She suddenly stopped when she saw the Shadow Man standing in front of her, blocking her path to Damian. She ran towards him. *He must have been responsible for the roller coaster.*

Rebecca rammed her elbow into his stomach, kicked him between his legs and kept on running towards Damian. She jumped just in time to throw him and herself out of the roller coasters way, as it crashed with a loud explosion.

Everyone ducked. The whole entire carnival was covered with pieces of the roller coaster and its tracks. The rest of the track fell, and the Shadow Man yelled as it crashed towards him. As the track crashed on him, a swarm of smoke enveloped the carnival.

Rebecca opened her eyes but then they closed and her body was swept into a dream where she stood face to face with the girl from her nightmares - Tanya. She looked sad, but also very happy as she spoke silently. "He almost got us again Rebecca. I guess I have got to be more careful. I think it's about time you took some of your own advice. Follow your feelings Rebecca. Follow them and you will get all of your answers."

Rebecca smiled at Tanya and then nodded her head. She felt warm and energized and also…

"Ouch. Watch it!"

The nurse pricked a needle into her arm. She woke up to see David, Damian and Julie in separate beds in the same hospital room. Rebecca asked the doctor how her other friends were, and he said that they were fine.

She was relieved that everyone was all right and she slowly drifted back to sleep. Her mind drifted off. *I can't believe that I ran past the Shadow Man like that. I never knew I had all that strength in me but somehow I feel that it was not my strength. But why?*

CHAPTER 8

Lana and the others waited outside the examination room for some news about Rebecca's sudden sleeping problem. It seemed that she was drifting off to sleep an awful lot; more than usual. And, as a result, she was sleepwalking even more. The doctor came out and told everyone that Rebecca was going to have to stay the night and take some tests.

Lana couldn't stand being in the hospital, so she decided to go skating, and Cathy went with her. The others wanted to wait for Rebecca to complete her tests so that they could see her. Victoria called her aunt and told her about the dreadful events that had taken place after their meeting with her. Madame Mystique asked if Rebecca was okay and said that she would be right over.

Lana skated gracefully on the ice of the local pond. During winter it was the greatest place for skating. Cathy was tired, so she sat on the bench and used Rebecca's cellular phone to call the hospital and find out how Rebecca was.

The doctor told the others that she was fine and that Madame Mystique was going to meet Rebecca. She decided that she needed to be there for her friend, so she asked Lana if she wanted to come as well, but Lana said no. Cathy got into her car and drove to the hospital.

Madame Mystique arrived at Rebecca's room and was let in by Julie. Everyone apologized for being skeptical, including Rebecca, who also said that she wanted to do a past life regression.

Lana skated peacefully unaware of the dark shadow that watched her. *I hate girls who think they are too hot.* Lana skated until she heard a crack coming from the ice. The Shadow Man laughed evily to himself, remembering how he had pulled out the sign that was beside the rink, warning skaters of the thin ice on the pond.

Madame Mystique dimmed all the lights in the room and lit several candles. Rebecca was told to breathe in and out slowly and relax. "Relax Rebecca. Breathe in and breathe out. I want you to picture yourself in a cave. In the cave there will be a clock. I want you to make the clock go backwards. I want you to walk backwards. A white light will envelop you to protect you. I want you to let your mind take you to wherever it is comfortable."

Rebecca listened to Madame Mystique's words and followed her instructions, following the path backward in the cave. The clock was going backwards when Madame Mystique spoke again. "You will hear my voice and only my voice alone. I will guide you through, but you have to tell me everything you see, hear, taste, and smell. I need description."

Rebecca nodded her head and was suddenly surrounded in a rush of warm white light. She felt so safe. The clock stopped and she suddenly fell out of the light and landed on the floor. She opened her eyes and smelled the scent of strange perfume.

"Rebecca, where are you?"

Rebecca heard a voice but ignored it, but she was speaking out loud anyhow. "I smell a scent of sun flower perfume. I am in my old bedroom."

David's eyes perked up and Madame spoke again. "Your room; describe it Rebecca."

Rebecca stood up in her room and saw the old antique mirror. She smiled and walked in front of it. She was dressed in her elegant white silk dress and her hair was loosely curled. She was herself again - she was Tanya.

***

Lana heard more cracks in the ice and started to scream, as the ice beneath her began to break under her weight. She tried to move but it was too late - she fell through the ice and into the cold water.

***

Rebecca spoke. "I can't believe I am back in my room. I feel so alive. But then again I feel so dead as well. I'm so tired."

Madame Mystique tried to make sense of what Rebecca had been saying. "Rebecca, why are you tired?" She smiled. "That is so simple my dear Madame, I am tired because I just came back from the ball. I am famished as well and my bodice is on too tight. I think I might faint."

Julie looked at Victoria and mumbled. "Bodice?"

Victoria shook her head and continued to listen on. Rebecca was now prancing around in her bedroom. *I am so happy to be alive. But wait what is the time.* The clock on her wall read 8.55pm. The date on her calendar was March 2nd, 1947. Rebecca spoke aloud, describing everything that she was doing and seeing, hearing and smelling.

She was startled when a man wearing a dark hood and clothes entered her bedroom. She stood up and began to yell at the man.

"What are you doing here? How did you get in here?"

The man looked at her and then began to snicker. "Do not be silly, Tanya. I told you that I would someday come back for you to reclaim the right I have on you. I love you."

"But I don't love you. I could never love you. I will never love you. You are a repulsive man. I am ashamed to even be associated with a scoundrel such as you. I suggest you leave."

The man's face grew tense and twisted in anger. He raised his fists. "If you wont be mine, you wont be anyone else's. I will have you. You will always be mine."

The man walked menacingly towards her. Before she could even scream, his strong hands pushed her into the direction of the window. *Oh no. Not again.*

"Help me!"

David and the others could hear her cries for help, but her voice seemed different - softer, mature.

***

Lana tried to get up but she kept slipping back into the water. Cathy had forgotten her purse so she drove back to the pond where she saw Lana. She got out of her car and ran towards the skating rink, but slipped and fell. She rammed into the ice, and she, too, fell into the cold water. The ice continued to crack when a couple spotted the two girls and went to help them.

***

Rebecca screamed for help. Madame Mystique tried to wake her but she could not. Rebecca tried to run out of the room, but the man pushed her, once again, against the wall towards the window. She screamed just as he gave her the final push, and she went hurdling towards the window.

Her body felt the impact of the glass and the pain of the shards penetrating her skin. Blood leaked out from her wounds and her screams echoed throughout the street of Peacefulville. She started to descend towards the ground.

But before she reached her final resting-place, she woke up out of her trance. She got up from her bed and looked around. Madame Mystique and the others looked at Rebecca. "Are you okay?" Julie sat next to David and squeezed his arm, as a worried look spread across her face.

Madame Mystique smiled uneasily and then walked over to the bed and spoke to Rebecca. "Rebecca, are you all right? Do you know who you are? Or where you are?" Rebecca sat for a few minutes and then she smiled and began to speak.

"Well of course I know who I am and where I am. My name is Tanya Annabella Arkenson and I am in Maple Crescent Hospital. The date is March 2nd, 1947…"

Everyone made a shocked expression. Suddenly Rebecca stopped what she was saying. *Oh no. It can't be true. I can't actually be Tanya.* She began to cry. *It is true.* The truth was out, and now she knew that she was Tanya. All the nightmares that she had been having weren't just nightmares. They were fears mixed with memories and warnings.

Rebecca spoke to all the others calmly, sounding somehow different. "Look, I do now know who I am. I am Tanya, or at least I was. I am so sorry that I put all of you in terrible danger. That man from my past, the one who killed me, is the same man here in this present - the Shadow Man."

Rebecca was interrupted when suddenly the doctor came running in with news that Lana and Cathy were both rushed into the hospital. Rebecca lept out of her bed and ran into the emergency ward.

Everyone else followed, as the doctor told them that Cathy was okay but Lana was in very serious condition. Rebecca started to cry. "It is all my fault that this is all happening." She wailed as she ran out of the hospital. Madame Mystique and David ran after her.

She was running across the parking lot when she suddenly stopped, and turned around to see a black car. In the car she saw a familiar person - someone from her past. But she could not see his face - it was covered by his black trench coat. He raced the car into her direction.

David saw the car speeding towards her, so he ran and managed to get her out of the way. Madame Mystique helped the two back to their feet. David looked at Madame Mystique and then to his Rebecca.

"Who was that? Rebecca, do you know who killed you?" Rebecca tried to remember her murderer's face, but she could not. She started to cry as David picked her up and led her back into the hospital accompanied by Madame Mystique. She still had things to say to Rebecca - important things.

Lana finally stabilized and was allowed to have visitors. Rebecca went inside to see her friend. Adam also arrived at the hospital with Detective Michaels. David told him about what they had just found out. Adam didn't want to believe a word he said, but he knew that there wasn't really anything else to believe. He would still have to see the Shadow Man for himself before he truly believed the story.

Lana looked like death, she was so pale - pale like a ghost. Rebecca went to the side of the bed and held her hand, and then left the room. Everyone was sitting outside, so she made an announcement.

"I am sick and tired of this. I now know that I used to live as Tanya, and now that I have my memory back, I vow that I will find out who my killer is and destroy him once and for all. I will find out the secrets of my past. This is Tanya's vow."

A chill ran down everyone's spines. They had never heard Rebecca speak with such anger and determination before. They were sure that she was now not the same girl anymore. Rebecca walked to a mirror and looked at herself. *Now if only I had my dress and my locket. Then and only then will I finally be my old self. Then that Shadow Man has no chance of surviving my wrath when I find out who he is. He is going to be sorry he ever crossed me. Very sorry.*

CHAPTER 9

The snow began to fall more heavily than usual, and Rebecca watched the snowflakes glide gracefully to the ground. They reminded her of gentle angels flying down to grace the earth with their presence. She was reminded of a time in her past when she, as Tanya, would sit on her sofa and watch the snowfall. She smiled at the warm memory.

She got up from the window and decided to do something that she had not done in a long time. She put on her long winter coat and gloves, left her room and walked outside. Once there, she began to dance around in the snow, letting the small flakes caress her face.

She felt so free. She felt whole once again. *I am back and this time I will be ready for you Shadow Man.* Julie came out of the bathroom and noticed that Rebecca was not in the bedroom, so she looked out of the window to see if Rebecca's car was still in the parking lot. Instead she saw Rebecca prancing and dancing around like she was some sort of princess.

Julie was surprised since she knew that Rebecca hated the snow. She did not mind watching it, but she hated actually being in it. Cathy saw Julie looking out of the window. She came over to see what was going on. She, too, spotted Rebecca.

"Look at her. She is not the same person anymore. She's more gentle and graceful." Julie agreed with Cathy. They watched her dancing in the snow and listened to her laughter. Victoria heard someone laughing, so she looked out her bedroom window and saw Rebecca. *She has really changed. I wonder if I should go and talk to her. Wait, today is December 18th, it's Rebecca's birthday. I totally forgot. Maybe a party will bring her back to normal.* Victoria walked to Rebecca's dorm room and knocked on the door. Cathy was surprised to see her. She sat down and told them her plans for Rebecca's birthday. They had also forgotten. Everyone forgot, distracted by all the horrible things that were happening, including Lana's most recent accident.

Rebecca stopped prancing around. She was getting cold now and wanted to go talk with her friends. She knew that they might still be worried about her. *Poor Lana, having to stay in the hospital for a few weeks.*

Rebecca walked into her room to find a surprised Cathy, Victoria, Julie, Jared, David, Jonathan and Fred gathered around her bed. "What's going on here?" Everyone smiled and made excuses. *Something is fishy.* Her sixth sense was speaking to her.

Madame Mystique had told Rebecca that she was psychic, but she could hardly believe what she heard. Now she believed, but it was hard to use her new found powers because she was inexperienced. It was not like she knew when she would have a feeling, or a vision. The feelings and the visions would just come and go. Also, she was told that she could move objects by using her mind, but she didn't know how she did it. She hoped that Madame Mystique would teach her.

Victoria got up from the bed and escorted Rebecca out.

She told her to put on a nice dress because everyone was going out to eat, and Cathy had to go to a model shoot. Rebecca already knew what she wanted for her birthday, and she also knew where to get it. She got her keys and told everybody that she was going to go and get a few things.

Rebecca drove until she spotted the old antique shop. She parked the car and got out of her car. The air was cold, and she shivered a little and walked towards the front door. She stopped and looked around - *nothing*.

She shook her head and walked through the entrance of the antique shop. A bell rang and a short, old man, with a few miscellaneous strands of hair on his head, came running out from the back room. Rebecca smiled and then walked up to him.

The man looked at her and asked if he could help her. She pointed to a breathtaking white silk dress that hung on the wall's display. She knew that the dress belonged to her. Of course Rebecca had no idea what happened when she died, but she was certain that the dress was hers. The man pulled down the dress from the display and then put it in a nice bag for her.

She grabbed the bag and then telephoned David from her cellular phone and asked if it was all right for her to come back home. David told her to meet everyone at Hotel Fritz. *Hotel Fritz. I wonder what they are all up to. Oh well, they are going to be surprised.*

Everyone was waiting at the Hotel Fritz, when Rebecca arrived, wearing an elegant silk dress - the same dress she had on the day she died, as Tanya. David looked up and down her body. He had never seen her look so amazing. "Where did you get that dress?"

Rebecca smiled at him. "I don't kiss and tell, lover boy." David blushed a little. She was even a little more playful, and he liked it. Damian was also going to be joining everyone.

Julie found out what level the special ball was on, and everyone got into the elevator. Jeremy looked at Rebecca feeling a bit uneasy, after what happened the last time that they were in an elevator together.

"Don't worry Jeremy. We won't fall down. I know." Jeremy looked at Rebecca, who winked at him. He then looked at Cathy, who was wearing a black dress that clung to her body like a snake to its prey. She looked amazing. Her shoes were made from snake skin. Her hair was braided. He was so happy that Cathy had been accepted to be a model.

Julie looked very stunning as well. She was wearing a short

white dress with ruffled sleeves. Jonathan looked good in his blue pants and his navy blue vest, and Victoria looked like a queen in her long satin gown. But, out of everyone, Rebecca was the best dressed.

She was surprised that her dress did not have any bloodstains on it. The last thing that she remembered was dying in that dress and now it was like nothing even happened.

The elevator finally stopped at its final destination. Everyone got out and waited to be seated. Once they were, the waiter came to the table to take everyone's orders.

"And what would you like Mon Cherie?"

Rebecca looked at the waiter. He was cute, in a boy next door kind of way. "My dear good man, I shall have Chicken Pasta and a glass of Chardonnay. Thank you."

David almost choked on his water. Rebecca never drank in her life and suddenly, she wanted a glass of Chardonnay. But then he remembered that Tanya was from a time where everyone drank Chardonnay. Julie and Jonathan smiled at one another.

Victoria told the waiter to go and get the surprise that they had ready for Rebecca. He came out holding a beautiful, gigantic, vanilla cake with pink and red flowers decorated around it. But the name on the cake wasn't right - it was not right at all.

The cake read, "Happy 18th Birthday, to Tanya." The cake was supposed to say, "Happy 18th Birthday to Rebecca." Victoria was upset, but Rebecca didn't seem to mind. She was happy, but Victoria looked nervously at the others. She had a suspicion that the Shadow Man was near by, but Rebecca did not seem to be having any sort of warning, so everyone thought it was okay.

Victoria gave Rebecca her present. It was a picture of all her friends in an elegant frame. Rebecca cried out with joy and gave her friend a hug. Cathy and Jeremy both bought Rebecca two tickets for a relaxation spa. Julie and Jonathan gave her a silk scarf. Rebecca loved silk. Jared gave her a birthday card, and Fred and Lana gave her a ring with her initials on it.

David was the last person to give her a gift. He gave her a pair of diamond earrings. She almost choked. *Diamond earrings.* Rebecca was so excited that she put them on. She looked stunning. She gave David a big, loving kiss.

Music started to echo through the ballroom and couples began to get up and dance. Of course, everyone looked very odd because they were dressed up in costumes. Hotel Fritz was a 24-hour masquerade ball. Everyone was dressed up in some weird, yet enchanting get up. David and the others all got up and started to mingle and dance. David kissed Rebecca's hand and then danced with her. She felt so good dancing in his arms.

She felt that she was dancing with her Jack again. David stopped dancing when the music stopped and decided to change partners and dance with Julie. Victoria excused herself to go to the bathroom. A handsome man approached Rebecca. Well, she could not see his face but she knew he was handsome - she just had a feeling.

Rebecca started to dance with the man., but abruptly stopped. Her head was starting to spin and an image of Victoria came into her mind. *She is going to be the Shadow Man's next target. I must find her.* Rebecca hurriedly ran off to find Victoria.

Victoria washed her face. *What is wrong with her? I thought she would get back to normal but I was wrong. I wish I could do something more for her.* Victoria swore when her bag fell to the floor. She bent over to pick it up when she saw a shadow of a man inside the washroom.

Oh no. Not him. Victoria had no choice but to hide in the stall. As the shadow walked towards her, she closed her eyes and prayed. The sound of the door made her open her eyes again. The man was gone. She left the stall and started to head back to the table, but was stopped when a hand covered her mouth.

It was the Shadow Man. He dragged her into the balcony, threw her against the wall and locked the door to the balcony. Victoria screamed, but it was no use - she could not be heard over the loud music.

The Shadow Man just stood there and faced Victoria. "Who are you? Why are you trying to hurt Rebecca? Why don't you leave us alone?"

The Shadow Man started to walk swiftly towards her. He grabbed her throat and lifted her into the air. Her shoes fell off. *Help me!* He was about to throw her off the balcony, but then he remembered that Rebecca was eighteen today, which meant she was her previous age again. The Shadow Man let go of Victoria, and she fell to the floor. She looked at him, but he just turned around and started to walk back inside the ballroom. Victoria got up and slowly walked inside as well.

That was so close. I have got to tell the others. Victoria heard her name being called, so she turned around to see a worried Rebecca calling out her name. Victoria was so relieved to see her. She had to warn her. She started to run towards her but she was tripped. She looked up to see the Shadow Man. Before she could scream, he grabbed her by the throat once again and this time he smashed her into the wall, knocking her out. He then put her body back out on the balcony.

The Shadow Man then changed into a blue tuxedo - like the one he wore a long time ago. He had a red rose in his hand; a rose for his beloved; a rose for the girl who stole his heart thirty seven years ago, and had now returned. He grabbed his mask.

She could sense the killer. *He's here. He's here somewhere but where?* Rebecca kept on smiling but her eyes were wondering around. *Nothing.* The Shadow Man was so happy; he was so close to his beloved. An old, familiar tune began to echo throughout the ballroom. The Shadow Man approached Rebecca, and almost choked at the sight of her. She looked the same - the same hair, the same looks and now, the same dress. He longed to feel her smooth body against his skin.

Rebecca turned and accidentally bumped into him. He was startled. He shyly extended his hand to her, and she smiled at him. She felt oddly drawn to him, so she gave him her hand and the two began to dance. Their hands touched as he twirled her around. They danced so beautifully together - just as they did before.

David saw Rebecca dancing. He was shocked because Rebecca could never dance very well, and now she was so good at it. Julie admired her newfound abilities. She danced so elegantly more gracefully, like a princess - she looked beautiful. Cathy watched her. *Look at her dance. I have never seen her do that before with out tripping anyone.* Cathy was getting tired. She still needed to get her clothes from her office.

She looked at her watch. It was getting late and the building would probably be closing. *Good. At least I have a key for the elevator and my office. I can still go by myself. Victoria said she was going to come with me. I wonder where she is? Oh well, maybe I will ask Rebecca to come because she seems to be enjoying herself a little too much.*

The music stopped and Rebecca bowed to her dancing partner and then went back to her table. There at the table sat Cathy all alone. "Hey, why aren't you dancing?" Cathy looked at Rebecca and then with a relaxed reply she said, "I don't want to dance anymore. Actually I wanted to go to my office across the street and get my clothes for the modeling shoot. You want to come?" Rebecca thought for a moment. "Sure, let's go."

Cathy had her own office where she had worked part time as a model consultant. But now the tables were turned, and she was the model to be consulted. Cathy smiled to herself. *I'm so sexy that it hurts! For the first time I am doing something where I'm not competing with Rebecca.* It seemed to Cathy that everything she did was like a competition and Rebecca was the person she was always up against.

Cathy and Rebecca then left the party unaware that the Shadow Man was watching them leave. *So, Cathy is now a model is she?* The Shadow Man began to laugh. *That means her face means a lot to her.* The Shadow Man left. David was wondering what happened to Rebecca, when Damian arrived, a little late due to a flat tire on his car. He apologized for missing the birthday cake, and said that he had a present for Rebecca.

Victoria finally regained consciousness, and a woman helped her up. She remembered the attack. *Rebecca!* Victoria started to walk but she felt groggy, so the woman looked for some help. David heard her calling, so he came to see what had happened. That's when he saw Victoria. She had a large bump on her head that looked very sore.

He helped her up and then he told the woman to get some ice for her head. He then slowly asked her what happened. She told him about the attack and how suddenly the Shadow Man had left, but then attacked her when she tried to warn Rebecca. David was very worried, especially since Rebecca and Cathy had vanished.

Victoria moved her eyes away from David. A tear started to form in her eye. *I wish that man would leave Rebecca alone.* Victoria saw two familiar looking girls walking towards the building across from the hotel. *Wait.* Victoria squinted her eyes.

"David, look it's Rebecca and Cathy."

He looked towards where she was pointing, and saw the two girls walking towards the building. David's eyes then spotted a dark shadow walking closely behind the two. He looked carefully - it was the Shadow Man. David told Victoria to warn the others and he ran to the elevator.

"I have got to save them."

Cathy's office was on the twenty third floor, and Rebecca was afraid of heights - really afraid. She was quiet in the elevator, trying to remember if Tanya was also afraid of heights like she was. Madame Mystique told her that some fears that she had could have originated from Tanya. Rebecca could not remember much, only that Tanya was never afraid of anything. The elevator opened and the two girls got out.

They were on the twenty third floor. Victoria could see them from where she stood. The window blinds were wide open and the lights were turned on. It was the only level that the lights were on in the building. *What are they doing there?* Victoria did not see the dark figure that walked around on the same floor of the building.

Cathy got her dress ready for the shoot. Rebecca noticed two mountain climbing packs in the office, and thought it was a little strange. When she pointed to the packs, Cathy started to blush. "Jeremy and I go mountain climbing sometimes." Cathy was blushing because everyone knew that Cathy hated sports and mountain climbing was a major sport.

"Cathy, I just want you to know that you're a good friend to me." The words stung Cathy like a mosquito bite. It wasn't really what Rebecca said, but how she said it. She sounded snobby and almost a little sarcastic.

Cathy tried not to sound mad. "Thank you." Cathy was near the door and bumped into it. Cathy then saw a shadow of a man. But before she could even scream, The Shadow Man came walking into the office with his knife in his hand. Cathy looked up at him and screamed. Rebecca saw him and in an instance she froze. Suddenly, a wind blew into the room and the lights began to flicker on and off.

Cathy looked at Rebecca. She knew Rebecca was doing something but she didn't know what. The Shadow Man fell backwards and the door shut and locked. Cathy looked to see Rebecca about to fall over. The wind had stopped.

She ran over to her. Her pulse felt weak but then it was back to normal. "Come on, get up. We have to get out of here." Cathy helped

Rebecca to the phone but the phone was dead. There was no way out this time. She looked around the office for a weapon or a way out, and saw the air vent.

The air vent led to the office laundry shoot, which lead to the basement. It was the only way out of the building. Cathy ran over to the air vent and tried to open it but she could not. She looked at Rebecca. "Can you open this with your powers?" Rebecca looked unsure. "I don't know. I don't know how to use my powers yet. But I can try. Stand back."

Rebecca concentrated her mind on the air vent, but nothing happened. The Shadow Man found an axe and he began to break down the door. Cathy turned around and began to scream. "Hurry up Rebecca!" She tried again, but still nothing happened. The Shadow Man managed to break the door down and he saw the two girls standing near the vent. He walked towards them, axe in hand.

Cathy screamed. Rebecca closed her eyes and tried again. This time she got some results. Her powers managed to turn on the vent. A lot of air suddenly blew into the office, knocking Cathy into the wall. Rebecca also fell against the wall. The Shadow Man's axe fell out of his hand, and the girls ran out the door.

"So much for the vent." Cathy looked at Rebecca. Rebecca smiled. They opened the emergency stairwell escape and ran down the stairs. The Shadow Man walked into the elevator and began to descend.

Cathy and Rebecca knew that the Shadow Man would probably wait for them on the lowest level, so they got out on the second floor and ran to the nearest window. Cathy broke the window open and looked out to see Julie and the others, as well as a fire truck and the police.

Cathy got onto the ledge of the building with Rebecca not far behind. Rebecca looked at Cathy. "We can jump you know, it's not that high up." Cathy looked at Rebecca. "Are you insane? Did you forget you died from jumping out of a window? Plus I am not going to rip this dress. It cost me an arm and a leg." Rebecca started to laugh and then made a smart comment back to her.

"I didn't jump out of a window and die, I was pushed. Also, if you don't jump and the Shadow Man finds us it really will cost you an arm and a leg. Meet you down there Cathy."

Rebecca closed her eyes and jumped. Damian saw her falling towards the ground, and ran to where she would land in an effort to catch her. But instead, she fell right on top of him, and they both slammed on the ground. Rebecca looked up at Damian.

"Thank you for saving my fall." He looked at Rebecca with eyes full of passion and lust. "Never mind. I don't mind that you landed on me." Rebecca smiled. He was flirting with her, and for some reason, she didn't mind. For some reason, Damian reminded her of Jack as well. *Why is that,* thought Rebecca?

Cathy was still clinging to the building. Jeremy opened his arms. "Jump Cathy." She made a sour face. She was not going to jump but then she heard a noise. She let go of the ledge and jumped and Jeremy caught her. Everyone was safe.

David was walking around on the first floor of the building, wondering where Rebecca and Cathy were. He heard the elevator, and saw that it was coming from the twenty third level. *That must be Cathy and Rebecca.* David walked over the elevator and waited, but then decided to wait at the security desk, which was not far from the elevators.

The door opened and the Shadow Man came out. David's eyes opened wide with fear, but he did not see David hiding behind the corner of the security desk. The Shadow Man heard a noise, so he looked around and he spotted something at the security desk. He slowly walked towards the table, and David turned to hide beneath the table.

The Shadow Man stood right in front of where David was hiding. He held his breath. He noticed that the Shadow Man's shoelaces were untied.

Rebecca's head began to hurt.

The Shadow Man's laces began to tie a knot with one another by themselves. David had no idea what was going on. The Shadow Man started to walk away but he tripped on the tied laces.

He looked at his shoes and spotted David. He struggled to get up, but David had already gotten out from under the table and ran outside the building. He was safe. The Shadow Man untied himself and retreated. He needed to think of a new avenue of attack. He disappeared.

Victoria was badly shaken up by the attack, but overall, she was fine. Jared took her home and stayed with her all night. David took Rebecca back to his place, forgetting that Damian was going to be there as well. He was kind of upset that he found Rebecca in his brother's arms, but he knew that Rebecca would never betray him. But his brother would - he was going to have to keep a close eye on Damian.

Cathy decided to stay at Jeremy's and Jonathan took Julie home. Fred just stood there, but he was invited to stay at David's as well. Rebecca went into a deep sleep as soon as her head hit the pillow. Rebecca was still mad that her shoe could not be found. Adam had a squad car watch David's building and everyone else's.

Rebecca woke up feeling hungry. She walked into the kitchen and got a drink instead. The food in David's fridge seemed all too fattening to her. She drank a can of V8 Tomato Juice. She decided to take a long hot bath but someone was in the shower.

She spotted Damian lying on the sofa, wearing boxers and no shirt. Her heart skipped a beat. *He is cute.* Rebecca began to turn back to her room when she accidentally stepped on Fred, who was sleeping on the floor. She laughed and then apologized.

She realized that it was David who was showering so she decided to take her shower after all. She opened the washroom door and let herself in. She then knocked on the glass door. A frightened David slid the glass door. He shook his head and laughed when he saw Rebecca. Then his face turned red.

This was the first time Rebecca had ever seen David with everything off of his body. She slipped out of her robe revealing to David the body that he had longed for ever since he could remember. She got into the shower and slid the door shut.

"You know what I really want for my birthday?"

David looked at her. His eyes twinkled with hidden excitement. "No, what?"

Rebecca kissed David hungrily. The hot water poured over both of their bodies. David was in ecstasy. So was Rebecca. The steam engulfed the room. After an hour the two of them lay in the warmth of the bed, with a gigantic comforter covering their bodies.

David kissed Rebecca. "I love you Rebecca. I don't want to lose you." Rebecca had her eyes closed so David thought she had gone to sleep. He kissed a few more times and then went to sleep himself. She opened her eyes and turned around slowly to face him.

I love you too, David and there is no way you are going to lose me. I am going to start investigating. I will find out who killed me and when I do, they are history. Rebecca closed her eyes and went to sleep.

CHAPTER 10

Rebecca slept peacefully in David's arms, as her mind alternated between Tanya's and her own. She started to remember her past; if only she could remember the person who had killed her. Her body felt like it was floating in mid air. But then her body began to feel pain; pain, as if someone had been poking thousands of needles into her body.

Little drops of blood began to pour out of her body and shards of glass were caught in her skin. She started to cry out but no one could hear her. Her blood became a large puddle that surrounded her. Two hands rose up from the puddle and pulled her down into it. She sank into the bloody puddle and ended up back in her old bedroom in 1947.

She was wearing her white silk dress again. It looked as if it was brand new like the day she had bought it. She sat on her bed, and spotted her diary. *My diary. Why, of course!* Rebecca reached for her diary. She looked for the last page that she had written in.

"Let me see...Aha, yes. March 2nd 1947. Dear Diary. I am so terribly upset. My life feels like it has been shattered like a piece of glass. The love of my life has betrayed me. I saw him dancing away through out the night with another woman. I can not believe that my Jack would betray me after everything that we have been through..."

Rebecca paused a little trying to remember if what she had written had happened. Rebecca started to remember that day. "I remember..." Rebecca continued on. "Oh diary, what am I to do now? Without Jack I have nothing. I am nothing. I am alone again. Oh diary, I have been through so many horrible things in my life and I do not think that I can go on without a companion. Without a love. Without Jack. Maybe I should go and stay at Mount Berry Lodge in Crescent Point. I feel so safe and peaceful there. Then I can think things over. I am so scared though because I am afraid that he will find me. I hope he does not find me ever again. He has already torn my family apart...until tomorrow diary. Sincerely Tanya Annabella Arkenson.

Who was I talking about? Well, now I know where to go to find some answers. Rebecca awoke. She sat up in the bed, and heard David talking to someone in the bedroom. Rebecca saw Damian standing near the bed. He was wearing his boxers still but with a shirt. He saw that Rebecca had waken up, and gave her a smile.

David was not very pleased. He was still upset with Damian for hugging Rebecca, but he was also very frightened. He had a close call with the Shadow Man - too close. David got of bed, got dressed and escorted his brother out of the room. Rebecca got out of bed as well and went into the bathroom to take a long shower.

She was going to start her investigation, and she already knew where to start.

"Mount Berry Lodge in Crescent Point. That place is still around. Maybe I can find some clues there linking to my past."

Rebecca took her bath and got ready. She told David she had to go to work, so that he would not worry about her. Now that she knew who she was and what she was capable of doing, she wasn't afraid. At least not that much. There was one thing that she was afraid of and that was something that Madame Mystique had said.

"You know Rebecca. It is possible that you are not alone here. Meaning, since you died and came back there might be a slight possibility that maybe one of your old friends, or even your killer has come back like you as well. Who knows, maybe they have come back as one of your new friends? You never know. So beware of everyone. Use your intuition."

Rebecca shivered at the thought that out of her friends one could be the actual killer. *No, that couldn't be.* Rebecca knew that it could not because she would have felt it. Rebecca got into her car and drove off into the direction of the lodge.

Rebecca drove for almost two hours. The snow started to fall with all of its fury. The storm was unexpected, and she found it hard to drive with all of the ice patches on the road. But she kept driving as carefully as she could. Her head began to ache and flashes began to appear before her eyes.

She panicked because she could not concentrate on the road. The car began to fishtail, and she almost ran off the road, but managed to get back in control. Rebecca's eyes began to close. *No. No. Not now. I can't go to sleep. I can't...*

Rebecca's mind drifted off into a nightmare. The car began to fishtail more violently then before. She was back in her usual nightmare. In the nightmare now she was Tanya. Her body crashed through the window, and she felt the cold air sting her face as she fell towards the ground. Her dress was torn and had many shades of red covering it.

She hit the ground and felt her neck snap and her arm twist, but she was still barely alive. A strong pair of arms picked her body up from the ground, and a pair of warm lips caressed her bloody cheek. The arms then placed her body in the back seat of a car.

She never remembered this part before because she had never seen what happened after the fall. But wait. This is not supposed to happen to her. The newspaper said that her body had been found. She heard the car stop and the door opened. A man walked out, and she dimly opened her eyes to see him coming towards the back seat of the car. He opened the door and scooped her out.

He carried her body for about a half an hour until he abruptly stopped. Rebecca opened her eyes slowly to see a forest and a well. *An old wishing well. I know this place. I've been here before with my family many times.* The man threw Rebecca's lifeless body into the well. He then poured some gasoline in the well and lit a match.

But before he dropped the match into the well, he said a few words. "Too bad it had to end this way Tanya. Too bad. But at least I got my story." The man then dropped the match into the well and Rebecca started to feel her body burn. The pain was unbearable.

She suddenly awoke from her trance, just in time to see the truck coming right at her. She slammed on the breaks and started to steer the car out of the truck's way. Her car fell over the side of the road and crashed into a deep ditch, throwing her through the window shield.

An hour passed by before she awoke. Her body was cold and numb. Her nose was bleeding and so was her head. The car was on fire, and the snow had gotten deeper and heavier. She managed to get up. Her coat was drenched, and she was freezing cold.

There was no one on the road anymore and the nearest gas station was about ten miles away. The snow was starting to get worse and she could hardly see a thing. But she could smell food. She sniffed the air again. The smell of roasted chicken came through the air. Rebecca looked around but could not see anything.

She looked at the snow-covered sign. She could make out the words. "Welcome to Crescent Point." *I'm here,* thought Rebecca. *The lodge is not so far from here.* She got her purse and her scarf and gloves and walked through the heavy snow deep into the forest.

The forest was supposed to lead her to the lodge. She walked almost a mile when she heard a noise. She turned around to see nothing. She continued to walk until she heard a growl. She froze in her tracks. She looked to her side to see a wolf.

The Grey Wolf looked ferocious, and very hungry. "Oh no."

Rebecca tried to walk another way but she noticed that there were more wolves. She was surrounded. The wolves made a circle around her and howled and growled at her.

Rebecca took a chocolate bar out of her purse and threw it as far as she could away from her. The wolves did not budge. They could smell the blood from Rebecca's wounds. Rebecca took off her glove, which was covered in blood and threw it away. This time the wolves moved towards the glove.

As soon as she could see a clearing to run, she ran for her life, but the wolves began to chase after her. Rebecca screamed her loudest. She did not have any time to waste. She spotted the lodge - her long forgotten cabin from the past.

She ran to the door and opened it, then shut it and stayed still. The lodge was dusty and dark, with a smell of dust and decay. She was surprised that the door was easy to open. There was hardly any snow blocking the path. It looked as though someone had been living there; there was even a fire burning.

Rebecca was cautious now. *Someone has been here, but they don't seem to be here now.* She went towards the window. "I hope those wolves are gone." She couldn't see the wolves so she turned her back towards the window. The sound of glass breaking could be heard from within the lodge.

One of the wolves crashed through the window and attacked her. She was stunned. The wolf clawed her arm. Rebecca struggled with the beast. She grabbed a fallen piece of wood and smashed the wolf in the face.

The wolf yelped a little and then started to growl again. Rebecca started to back away from the wolf when she tripped over a loose floorboard. The wolf snarled and then jumped, ready to attack her.

Then another sound echoed throughout the lodge. The sound of a gun shot. The wolf fell to the ground, at first growling, but then crying in agony and pain. Rebecca looked back to where the shot come from. A young woman stood in the hall. In her hands she carried a rifle. Her hair was golden yellow and the length was to her shoulders. Her eyes were blue.

The girl was very pretty. Rebecca tried to speak, but her eyes were starting to hurt. Her vision got blurry and then she fainted. The woman checked Rebecca's wounds, which looked like they were foaming. She picked Rebecca up and took her to her house, to treat the cuts and scratches.

CHAPTER 11

Rebecca was trapped in a nightmare, running away from a pack of wolves. They looked hungry and she was their meal for the day. She screamed as she ran from them. She kept on running until she could not continue. The ground beneath her began to shake.

Rebecca looked behind her and saw that the wolves had disappeared. Relieved, she slowly walked through the woods until she spotted a well. It was the same well that she had seen in her vision. She walked towards it, afraid of what she might find. She looked into it, but saw nothing but water.

The water was stagnant and a muddy brown. She continued to look into the well, in total confusion. *I don't remember getting thrown into the well after I died. That's not how it happened. I know. I have read the articles. My body was found by the police but then why did that man say at least I got my story. How peculiar.*

Rebecca's eyes widened as two bony hands followed by a whole body rose from the water. She screamed at the sight of the disgusting body that smelled of decay. She turned around and began to run but a voice stopped her. The voice belonged to the rising corpse.

Rebecca turned around to face a beautiful girl. The girl was so familiar to her. She stared at the girl, and her voice trembled. "Do I know you?" The girl just stared at her for a few moments, but then, in a kind and sweet voice ,began to speak.

"It's me, Tanya. Isabella. Your friend from long ago. The body that was dumped in that well was mine not yours. The reason you had a vision of yourself getting brought to this place is because I needed to talk with you."

Rebecca went over to her friend and gave her a hug. *Isabella. I remember her. She was such a nice friend. But she had disappeared a few weeks before I was murdered.*

"Isabella, do you know who murdered me?" Isabella looked away from Rebecca. Her eyes began to glisten with drops of tears. "All I remember was that I was killed because I had learned a secret of your past that I was not supposed to know. Others knew it as well but they did not last so long."

Rebecca looked at Isabella. "Others?" Isabella nodded her head. "Others, such as Amy, Steven, your sister Christina, and even Jack." *Jack.* Rebecca was surprised at what Isabella had said. "Did you say sister? You mean I had a sister. Who was she? Where is she? What happened to her?"

Isabella started to laugh out a little. "You never changed a bit, did you, Tanya. You are still the same girl. Yes, you did have a sister and she loved you very much. When your parents died, she moved out with her husband. After that I don't know what happened."

Rebecca's eyes started to fill with tears. *I had a sister. Wait. That must be the reason that I started to get a headache when David was mentioning Damian. I was probably having a memory of my sister but it didn't surface. But now I think that I am starting to remember her.*

She started to remember her sister. Her name was Christina. She was older by three years. Christina looked much like Tanya did, but she had long brown hair and hazel eyes. Her body type was a little different - healthier looking. *I miss her.*

"What happened to the others?" Isabella looked at Rebecca sadly. "Well, Amy died a few weeks after you did. She got very sick. Steven was married and left Peacefulville and Jack...well, Jack disappeared. No one knows what happened to him."

Rebecca was so upset that Amy had died at such a young age and that her Jack had disappeared. *Maybe Jack is the man who is stalking me. That couldn't be true. How about Steven? Who knows?*

Rebecca started to fade away, so she said goodbye to Isabella. Her eyes opened, but the light in the room made her eyes hurt. A few minutes later, she was able to open her eyes, and sit up. She was in a bedroom of some kind. Her arm killed. She looked at her arm to see that all her cuts and scratches were bandaged up.

She stood up and tried to think of the last thing that happened. "Let me see, I remember the wolf attacking me then there was that woman..." Rebecca heard voices coming from the hallway, so she walked towards the door and looked outside. No one in sight. She walked cautiously down the hallway until she saw a room with a light on.

She walked into the room and saw Julie and Victoria sitting on the sofa talking to the woman who saved her. Victoria saw her and ran to her side. "Hey there. Are you okay?" Rebecca looked at her and started to cry. Julie walked over to her as well.

"You gave us a scare, you know that, Becky." Julie said, in a worried tone. Rebecca gave her a hug as well. "But how did you find me?" Julie explained to Rebecca that the woman who had saved her had found the phone book that was in her purse.

Rebecca got it now. She then turned her eyes to the woman. "Thank you." The woman smiled at her. "Your welcome. My name is Dina. Dina Mills. Nice to meet you Rebecca. You know what? You are one brave girl."

Dina told Julie and Victoria about the wolves and the girls were shocked. They were stuck up there for awhile; the snowstorm made driving impossible. Rebecca was glad because she still needed to go find that well; the well that Isabella was buried in.

Maybe there is a clue. Maybe. Well at least I know that my body was found, but poor Isabella. Rebecca sat down on the sofa beside Victoria. The four girls began to talk with each other. A sudden noise of someone upstairs made them stop.

Julie looked at Dina and whispered, "What was that Dina?" Dina put a finger on her mouth. Julie understood and kept quiet. Dina got up and walked towards the stairs. Julie, Victoria and Rebecca followed as well. Dina walked up the stairs until she got to the room in which the noises were coming from.

She then smashed the door wide open. A man was standing in the middle of the room, wearing a ranger's jacket, with a long knife in his hand. The girls all began to scream. Dina did not scream, recognizing her friend, Peter. She calmed the girls down and then introduced them to Peter.

"...And last but not least, Peter meet Rebecca." Rebecca looked at the man and then she noticed something. *I know him. He's...He's...Peter. Peter Carmel. He's my best friend's little brother.* Rebecca looked at him again. Peter looked old, very old. Too old. But still, she remembered him.

Peter looked at her. He thought that his eyes were betraying him. *It can't be.* His voice trembled. "Is that you Tanya?" Peter then fainted. Rebecca looked at Victoria with her eyes wide open. Dina looked at the fainted Peter and then to Rebecca.

"What was he talking about?"

Peter still had not woken up. He slept uncomfortably on the couch. Dina and Julie sat and watched him sleep. They hit it off great. Julie liked to talk to interesting people and Dina was very interesting. Victoria and Rebecca went upstairs to take a nap. It was close to midnight but it hadn't reached midnight just yet. Victoria couldn't sleep, so she also joined the two girls in the living room.

Rebecca twisted and turned in the bed, as horrible visions and thoughts invaded her mind. *The well. I have to go to the well.* Rebecca got up from her bed. Her eyes opened, in a zombie like trance. She stood up and started to walk downstairs. She was sleepwalking again.

Julie spotted Rebecca and called out to her but she kept on walking down the stairs with slow and steady strides. That's when she noticed her eyes. "Oh no, Becky is sleepwalking again." Dina looked and saw her walking towards the door. Before the girls could stop her, she opened the door and walked out into the storm in search for the well.

Dina and the others hurriedly put on their clothes and went after her. Dina looked at the two girls and jokingly said, "What is this? 'The Rebecca Walks at Midnight,' or something? Does she sleep walk a lot?" Victoria answered. "Yes, and she's getting worse."

Dina told Victoria not to worry. Peter suddenly awoke. He saw the door wide open, and he knew that Tanya must have gone to the well; her well. He was very old but he still had love for Tanya. She was like his0 sister. Peter got up and put his coat on and ran outside in the direction of the well.

Rebecca kept on walking. A wolf spotted her and followed. It suddenly leaped out of the bush and ran towards her. Julie spotted Rebecca and then the wolf, but Dina didn't have her gun with her. Victoria started to shout out to her but it was useless. Julie covered her eyes.

The wolf jumped towards her, but Rebecca only saw the well. She was only a few feet away from it. The wolf came at her with fury. Rebecca grabbed a hold of the wolf's neck, and then, with one yank, she broke it. She then flung the poor creature aside like a toy. Dina's face grew full of shock and terror. She had never seen a person kill a ferocious beast without a weapon.

Julie could not believe it either. Victoria threw up at the sight of the dead wolf. There was definitely something wrong with Rebecca. She walked towards the well and stopped to look down into the frozen water.

Rebecca stepped into the well and dropped herself in. Victoria saw her fall, and ran after her. The others ran with all their might. Rebecca was standing on top of the ice, talking to herself. She had fallen a little too deep. The girls looked down at her, and saw the ice beneath Rebecca begin to break.

Julie screamed, knowing that if they did not get Rebecca out of the well, she would fall through the ice and die. Julie pulled off her scarf and yelled at her to grab it but Rebecca ignored her. The ice broke and she fell through. The girls screamed.

Rebecca was submerged with ice cold water. Her eyes scanned the floor of the well until she spotted a ring. She managed to pick it up.

Peter arrived on the scene. He told the girls to take a hold of the rope while he got into the well and tried to get her out. He managed to grab a hold of Rebecca who was now unconscious.

The girls quickly got her home. Dina rushed down stairs with blankets and she brought some hot water. Rebecca started to shake and quiver, still in deep sleep. Awhile later, and much to everyone's relief, she opened her eyes.

Dina noticed the ring in her hand. "Did you get that from the well Rebecca?" She looked at the ring in confusion and then, suddenly, she had a vision of the ring. In the vision she could see the owner of the ring. He was wearing it the day Isabella was killed. It was also worn by the man who pushed her out of her bedroom window.

Concentrate Rebecca. She tried her best, and finally the image of the man who had pushed her from the window appeared in her mind. She couldn't believe who she saw. It was a man from her past; a man that she had trusted with her heart; man whom she thought was her friend. The man was none other then...

"Rebecca, Rebecca." Rebecca came back to reality. Julie and Victoria stood by one another. "What is it Rebecca? Did you have another vision?" Dina looked at Julie. Rebecca stammered. "I know who killed me. I saw his face. I can't believe this. The man who killed me was Steven Lancaster. My best friend."

Julie and Victoria looked at one another. Dina looked confused. "What is going on?" Rebecca sat down on the couch and began to cry. Julie and Victoria sat down beside her and began to tell Dina everything.

Dina was shocked and also fascinated. She really didn't know what to believe. "So you're saying that this Shadow Man guy is the guy who has been stalking you and your friends and now he is trying to kill you….again?" Rebecca looked at Dina and nodded her head. Dina sat down.

She was quiet for a while, but then she got up to speak. "Rebecca, if there is anything that I can do to help let me know. I am your friend now, you know. Friends stick by one another." Rebecca got up and gave Dina a hug and then she gave Peter a hug. He was shocked at the news as well.

"Looks like the Shadow Man has been found out. He can't keep chasing after you, now that you know who he is."

Rebecca agreed with Dina, but then she didn't know if it was Steven after her. It could be anyone from her past life. Maybe one of them came back, just like she did.

"Maybe, but I need proof that he's still alive."

Julie and Victoria stood up. "Well if it's proof you need, we will help you get it." Rebecca smiled. "Looks like the Shadow Man is up against more then he bargained for. He's toast."

CHAPTER 12

Rebecca, Julie and Victoria left the next morning. The snow had stopped and the roads were clear. Dina told the girls that she would be coming to visit them in town and would do anything to help them. Rebecca wore the ring she had found. It was a good tool to link her to the killer. With it she would be able to track him down easier.

When they all arrived back home, David, Jonathan and Jared sat patiently in the dorm room. All three were pretty mad that the girls had been missing for practically the whole night.

When David saw Rebecca, his eyes filled with worry. He was mad, Rebecca could tell, but instead of yelling at her, he embraced her in a warm hug. She was surprised. She thought he was going to yell at her. Instead, he just asked her what happened. She didn't answer him.

Rebecca had told Julie and Victoria not to say a word to anybody because she didn't know who the killer was yet, and it could be anyone. She wanted to use caution. The girls understood and swore not to say a word to anyone. Jared and Jonathan waited for an explanation of where all three were the whole night.

Victoria explained that Rebecca had a little accident and she had called them to come get her, but they got snowed in and they all had to seek shelter at the nearest house. The guys nodded their heads. Rebecca decided to take the first step in making sure that she and the others remained safe. She telephoned her work and told her boss that she quit.

Rebecca wanted to go to talk to Adam, and Victoria and Jared decided to go with her. David went to the auto shop to get his car checked. It was a slow day at the shop, so Parker, the mechanic, took David's car in and told him it would only take about forty-five minutes.

David was sitting patiently in the waiting room when he heard shouts. He walked into the garage, and saw Parker dead on the ground. He shivered and looked around, knowing who the culprit was. Rebecca had told him earlier that Steven had killed her when she used to live as Tanya.

David slowly looked around, but there was no sight of anyone. "Come out from wherever you are, Shadow Man, or should I say, Steven Lancaster." David waited, but no one was in sight.

The Shadow Man emerged from David's car, carrying a long metallic rod in his hand. He walked towards him, raised the rod up high and got ready to strike David, who had his back to him. The Shadow Man spoke, "Who said I was Steven Lancaster?"

David whirled around but the Shadow Man smashed the rod into his head. The pain was incredible. David couldn't speak. He just fell to the floor and his eyes shut. The Shadow Man pulled out a card from David's coat pocket that read, Adam Carmicheal. The Shadow Man had found his next target; this time for death.

Rebecca, Victoria and Jared arrived at the bustling police station. Rebecca knocked on Adam's office door, and he answered it, surprised to see her. He let them all in and had them take a seat.

Rebecca told Adam everything that she had found out and asked him if there was any way he could help her. He suggested that maybe Rebecca should move and change her phone number, just until the police caught the Shadow Man. She thought that was a good idea, giving her more time to uncover her secrets and trace Steven's whereabouts.

Adam arranged for her to move into an abandoned house that was used to relocate people once in a while. Rebecca looked at the picture of the house. It was nice; nice and old. She noticed that in the background there was another old house; a house which was familiar to her; a house with a marble stone pathway leading towards the front entrance.

"My house. Adam, this house in the background is my old house. This is Tanya's house. I recognize it." Adam took the picture from her and looked at the photo carefully. He wanted to help Rebecca, but he didn't know if he believed in past lives, even though she seemed so sure.

"Well, if you'd like to stay in this house, I'm sure we can arrange it." A smile spread across her face. "Really. Oh, thank you Adam." He got a police escort to take her to the house. Victoria decided that she would stay with her, just in case, so Jared went home to get his clothes as well. He was not going to let Victoria stay by herself while the Shadow Man was loose.

Adam was filing some papers with his back to the door, when heard someone enter his office. "I'll be right with you in a minute." Adam looked up and smiled, but his smile quickly faded. A dark figure stood in front of him. His door was shut. "Tell me where you sent my Tanya?" Adam realized that the man was the Shadow Man.

Adam tried to get his gun, but he was stopped when a knife plunged into his chest. Adam stared down at his chest, covered with his blood. The Shadow Man shoved the knife harder, and he fell to the floor. The Shadow Man spoke again, this time more angrily than before. "Tell me."

The Shadow Man picked up the typewriter from the table, and walked over to Adam who was trying to get up. He saw the Shadow Man, but he couldn't move. He was paralyzed with fear. The Shadow Man raised the typewriter and smashed it into Adam's head. His skull made a cracking sound, and he stopped struggling and moving.

Rebecca called Fred on her cellular phone. She wanted him to come and stay with her as well, feeling that he might be of some help to her. He told her that he would meet her at the house. Victoria's mouth opened wide when she saw the house.

The house was amazing. There was a marble stone pathway leading towards the door. The house was so big. *Better than a mansion,* she thought to herself. She looked over at Rebecca who had tears running down her face. "My house. My old house..." Rebecca walked towards the front door, as happy and sad memories started to enter her mind.

Victoria silently followed her as she opened the door to her house. As soon as the two walked in, a breathtaking view surrounded them. There, in front of the door, was a spellbinding staircase made from exquisite oak, and paintings hung on the walls. Rebecca looked around in amazement. "Just like I remember it. Nothing has changed."

She ran up the stairs with Victoria right behind her. Rebecca stopped in front of a door with a beautiful design carved on it. Her hand shook as she reached for the door handle and opened the door. The room was breathtaking. To Rebecca, it was still the same as she had left it.

Victoria walked into the room and noticed how beautiful it was. There were cream colored silk curtains, and pastel violet bed sheets of silk, as well. "Beautiful." She was so amazed, but then she saw Rebecca's tear stricken face.

She had stopped in the middle of the room and was staring at the window - the window she had fallen from. Victoria walked over to her. "It's okay. You're alive again. Nothing is going to happen to you. Look, the window is brand new again too." The window had been replaced. Even though it had the same design, it didn't feel the same to Rebecca.

Victoria looked out the window, and saw that the drop was very high. *No wonder she died on impact,* she thought. She looked away from the window and noticed some sort of chain stuck in the vent below her feet.

"Rebecca, what is that chain in the vent?" Rebecca, who had been standing motionless, walked towards her and looked down. There, she saw something that she had not seen in many years. "Oh, my God. It's my locket." Rebecca got down on her knees and opened the vent. She then stuck her hand into the vent, and her fingers managed to get a hold of the chain.

She yanked it up and pulled out her locket. Nothing was broken. She couldn't believe it. It was the locket that was given to her by her parents on her eighteenth birthday thirty-seven years ago. Victoria took the locket from Rebecca's hand and looked at it.

The initials read T.A.A. Victoria thought for a moment. *That must stand for Tanya Annabella Arkenson.* She turned the locket around to read the inscription.

"To my darling daughter Tanya Annabella Arkenson. May you have all the happiness in the world. Always remember, we'll always be with you." Victoria looked at Rebecca. She couldn't believe it. It was true. The locket was proof.

Rebecca opened the locket and gasped. Victoria looked at the locket and gasped as well. There, in the locket, was a picture of Tanya. She was an exact replica of Rebecca. Beside her was a picture of a handsome man.

Victoria looked at Rebecca and asked her who the man was. "That'…That's…Jack. The love of my life." Victoria bit her lip. *Oops. I hope I didn't make her upset.* "I'm sorry Rebecca, I had no idea…" Rebecca looked at her. "That's alright."

The locket opened up again to reveal more individual photos of people. Rebecca recognized them all. There was a picture of Amy, Claudia, Peter, Samantha, and Daniel, Isabella and, last but not least, Steven. "That's the guy who killed me."

Victoria looked at Steven's picture. *He looks so familiar. I think I have seen him before, but where?* Rebecca wore her locket. Now she was truly whole, once again. She had her dress, her locket, her house and her memories.

Now if I only could find out something on Steven. Fred arrived with Jared, and both were amazed by the gorgeous house. They all decided to go for a walk around the neighbor hood, hoping to jog Rebecca's memory.

Rebecca got tired and decided to rest, but then she saw it. "It can't be…" The guys looked at what she was looking at. Rebecca was looking at a sign. The sign read Clevont Cemetery. Jared looked at her. "What? Did you remember something?"

She looked back at them all and answered, "That's the cemetery where I am buried." They all looked at one another in shock. Everyone walked into the cemetery. Rebecca looked all around until she spotted her grave.

Rebecca walked over to it. *I can't believe it. That's my grave.* Everyone walked around Tanya's grave, which was surrounded by flowers, remaining quiet. Rebecca started to remember.

"I am remembering a poem that Steven gave me. It was his favorite and it was also my favorite."

Victoria loved poetry. "Really, what was it?"

Rebecca concentrated and then she finally remembered. "I remember it. The title is, *Flowers on My Grave.* 'My life so full of sadness, there is nothing else to say, my feelings have been hurt, by every other day, but still do I stay happy, my heart a shallow cave, I'll always feel this sorrow, there are flowers on my grave.' That was by a guy named H. Singh. He was an Indian poet."

Victoria looked like she was out of breath. "That was beautiful." Fred started to laugh. "Yeah right. It was totally morbid." Rebecca looked at him. "Naive Fred. Of course you would think it is. It's supposed to be like that."

Fred looked at Rebecca, bewildered, but Jared just stood there and smiled. Rebecca noticed a red rose lying on her grave. She bent over and picked it up. Suddenly she felt his presence. It was definitely Steven's presence - he was there.

"Steven was here. Not too long ago. I know."

The others looked at her with worried expressions on their faces. Rebecca looked all around but then she remembered something; something that would lead her to Steven. *I'm coming Steven. You just wait and see what fate has in store for you after I am done with you.*

CHAPTER 13

Everyone sat around the table in the cafeteria. No one had heard from Rebecca, so David was surprised to see her walk into the cafeteria. She looked totally changed; like a different person; like Tanya. Rebecca walked over to the gang and sat across from David.

He was afraid to talk to her but he had been worried. "You feeling okay today Becky?" She looked at him strangely but then noticed the nasty bump on his head. "What happened to your head? Wait, let me guess. The Shadow Man attacked you." David shook his head. He was worried about Rebecca. He knew that the Shadow Man meant business.

Cathy was quietly staring at Rebecca. Rebecca noticed her looking at her. "Yes. Can I help you Catherine?" Cathy blinked her eyes a few times. *No one has ever called me Catherine before, except my mother.* "No." Rebecca smiled and then saw Julie watching her with fascination.

"Can I help you Julie?" Julie blinked here eyes and then responded. "No. I just like your new hair do, it's...its...so Tanya."

Rebecca smiled. "Thank you. I know. Isn't my hair great."

David looked at Jeremy, who could not believe that this girl who sat in front of them was the same girl that they all knew before. She seemed so different. Jeremy took a hold of Cathy's hand, and she looked at him and smiled.

Julie noticed that everyone was acting different, so she broke the silence. "So Tanya…I mean Rebecca. Sorry. What I was trying to say is that I was wondering if you finally learned how to use your sixth sense…"

Rebecca shook her head. "Not really. I haven't." Julie smiled a little and then looked to see Jonathan coming to the table with Damian walking beside him. She threw a piece of paper at David, who turned to see Damian.

"Oh, great." Rebecca stared at David, and suddenly she was in his mind. His thoughts echoed through her own thoughts, and she could hear what he was saying. He was jealous of Damian. He thought that Damian was a threat to their relationship. Rebecca knew that this was not true at all; she loved David too much.

Damian reached the table and walked to where Rebecca was sitting. But Rebecca did something to him, and he tripped on his own foot and fell, landing on poor Jared. David started laughing, as did everyone else.

Rebecca started to laugh, but then she got up. "Everyone, I must go. There are a few things that I must take care of, I will come and meet with all of you later on, though. Tottles."

She grabbed her purse and left the cafeteria. Everyone just stared at her. Cathy was shocked at the rudeness in her tone. David couldn't believe she had said "tottles." Julie noticed a paper on the floor. She picked it up. It had an address on it.

876 Maple Berry Drive. Lancaster Manor. Lancaster Manor. That's Steven's last name. Wait, Rebecca must be going to his house. I have got to stop her. Julie excused herself and ran out of the cafeteria. Fred saw Julie run out abruptly, so he also left to follow her.

Rebecca drove Victoria's Lexus up to a big house. "So, this is Lancaster Manor, eh?" She parked the car a few houses away, so that no one would see her car. She started towards the entrance, but then decided to walk around to the back.

She spotted an open window. *Perfect.* She looked around but didn't see anything, so she climbed through the window. "This is quite different; from falling out of windows, to climbing through them. What a twist," she giggled. *Snap out of it. You are here for an important reason. There is no time to giggle.*

She fell head first into the house, and quickly got up to see if anyone heard her fall, but there was no one in sight. "Thank God." She got up and started to walk around. *What a beautiful place. Not as nice as my place, but okay I guess. That is, of course, if you're a rich bastard who kills young girls by throwing them out of windows.*

Rebecca spotted a phone book and picked it up, as visions flashed through her mind. A vision of a young girl came to her. *I know her. That's...that's...*

Rebecca's thoughts were interrupted by a noise, and she ducked behind a closet. *Please go away.* Julie walked into the house slowly, trying not to make any noise. Rebecca dropped the address book and a piece of paper fell out. She quickly bent over and picked it up.

She unfolded the paper and saw that it had been written on. "StarLight Mental Health Facility. Wendy Lancaster." Rebecca could not believe it. "Wendy Lancaster. That's Steven's baby sister. Perfect."

Rebecca made a run for the window, crawled out and ran to her car. Julie heard her movements, so she hid in the corner. When she heard nothing else, she looked around to make sure that no one else was there. When she saw nothing, she started to walk again.

The Shadow Man walked down the stairs of Lancaster Manor and spotted Julie. *What is she doing here? It doesn't matter now.* Julie heard a noise coming from the door to her right, so she walked over to the door and opened it slowly. The door led to the basement.

She didn't know what to do, but she knew that Rebecca could be down there, so she built up her courage and went down the stairs. She didn't see anyone. She smiled to herself and then turned around to head back. The door to the basement was closed.

"I didn't close that." She ran up the stairs and tried to open the door but it was locked. "Shit." She didn't know what to do, so she decided to find a window in the basement. She walked back down the stairs and searched all the rooms.

She walked into a dark room. She couldn't see anything, so she tried to look for the light. She did see a chain., so she walked over to the chain and pulled it. The light in the room turned on. *That's much better.* She smiled and turned around. That's when the Shadow Man hit Julie across the face with a blunt object. She fell to the floor, and looked up to see the Shadow Man.

He grabbed Julie's feet and dragged her out of the room. He then picked her up with one hand and walked to another door. The door opened to an old wine cellar. The Shadow Man looked at Julie's face.

"I hope you like pets." He pushed her inside and locked the door. Julie slammed on to the floor. The light was on and it smelled bad - as if something had died. She got up to look around, and saw Dexter's dead, rotten corpse. She started to back away, but then she tripped over something.

She looked down and saw Adam, his head badly crushed. She began to throw up. *Help me someone! Help me!* Fred walked into the dark and horrid house. *Julie must still be here because her car is still in the driveway.* Fred saw an earring near the basement door, and picked it up. "This is Julie's." He opened the door to the basement and walked down the stairs. Julie heard a hissing sound. She sat down in the corner of the wine cellar and saw that Dexter's body was convulsing and shaking.

Julie started to scream, as Dexter's mouth began to open and a green lizard came crawling out, flicking its tongue. Julie screamed at the top of her lungs. She hated lizards. As the lizard crawled towards her, she grabbed a bottle of wine and smashed it on its head.

The lizard looked dead, but Julie heard more hissing and she turned to see five more lizards coming out of Dexter's mouth. Then she heard a different type of hissing. A snake emerged from behind Adam, and she began to shriek.

***

Rebecca walked into the mental institution, and found out where Wendy was. When she reached the room, she opened the door and walked inside.

A young woman in her mid thirties sat, rocking herself back and forth on her bed. The woman saw her and stood up. "Wendy, Wendy it's me. Tanya. I'm still alive." The woman looked at Rebecca with uncertainty, but then her face became happy. "Tanya. Steven's Tanya." She was relieved that Wendy remembered her.

"That's right. It's me. Oh, Wendy what happened to you? Where's Steven? I want to see him again." Wendy got up and then pulled out a scrapbook. Rebecca took the book and looked through it. Then she spotted an article. The headline read,

"Steven Lancaster, age twenty five, dies in brutal car crash."

Oh my God that means Steven's dead. Rebecca began to read the article. "Steven was grieving over the loss of his wife." *That's horrible.* Rebecca read on, but the article had nothing on Steven's wife. *I wonder who she was.* Rebecca gave Wendy a big hug and then she left. *If Steven is dead then the Shadow Man must be Jack.*

***

"Get me out of here. Please!" Julie banged at the door. She could feel the lizard crawl up her leg. Fred heard her shouts. He tried to open the door but the door would not open. "Don't worry Julie." Julie heard Fred's voice. "Fred. Fred is that really you?" Fred was glad to hear Julie's voice. "Yes."

Fred saw a crow bar on the floor. He then grabbed it and began to ram it against the door. He finally got the door open. There he saw the long snake wrapped around Julie. He struggled to get the snake off of her. He finally got it off. Julie hugged Fred. She had never felt so frightened in her life.

"The Shadow Man was here. We have to find Rebecca."

They made their way back up the stairs and to the car.

***

Wendy sat alone in her room. She rocked back and forth. A dark shadow began to cast itself against her wall. She looked up to see the Shadow Man. A frightened expression began to form across her face.

"No. No."

The Shadow Man grabbed Wendy by the neck and twisted it. The sound of her neck cracking made him feel so much better. Her body went limp in his arms. He then threw her on the bed. He saw the scrapbook on the floor. He picked it up and went through it. *Oh, all the bittersweet memories.*

***

David and Damian sat in their towels in the steam room. David was trying to relax, but it was difficult with Damian there. Damian noticed his evil glare. "Is something wrong, little bro?" David forgot that he was staring at his brother. "Naa. Not really." He got his clothes on and Damian then did the same.

"Look, if it's about Rebecca, then hear me, little bro. I will not interfere with you two."

David was glad that he didn't have to say anything; his brother understood. Jonathan and Jeremy suddenly entered the steam room, wearing shorts and a shirt.

"Hey."

David was surprised to see them. They all heard the door opening and looked towards the entrance, but there was no one there. David began to think about Rebecca again. *I wish we could have a talk. I miss her; the old her not the new her.*

A sound of something scattering across the ceramic floor made everyone stand up. "What the hell was that?" David shook his head in uncertainty. Suddenly, a swarm of scorpions came crawling towards them. "Holy shit." Jonathan was terrified of the scorpion's poisonous stingers.

The only way out was the front entrance, which was blocked by the scorpions. They all stood up on the bench. Damian was panicking. "Who would do something like this?" Jeremy looked at him. "You haven't met the Shadow Man have you?" Damian looked confused.

David managed to grab his pocket knife that had fallen to the floor. He had an idea, but he did not know if it would work. He began to stab one of the pipes that had steam running through it and punctured it. A wave of steam came out of the pipe, and the scorpions began to walk everywhere.

Damian slipped and fell off the bench and the scorpions began to walk towards him, with their stingers ready to attack. He began to yell, but just then, the steam room began to shake. The lights began to flicker on and off and the scorpions that were near Damian flew violently into the wall.

A gush of air came into the room, and a piece of electrical wire broke and came down from the ceiling and landed on the floor. It started to move towards the scorpions and drove them out of the steam room, allowing them to escape. They ran out of the steam room as fast as they could, being careful not to step on one of the scorpions.

They spotted Rebecca outside the building, her hair flowing in the air. A young woman stood next to her and then, just down the street, came Julie and Fred. David couldn't take his eyes off of Rebecca. She had saved them. *So she lied to Julie when she said she didn't know how to use her powers. But why?*

Rebecca's powers began to fade and then the wind stopped. She started to get dizzy and fell to the floor. David ran to her. Her pulse weakened, but then returned to normal. Rebecca looked up into David's eyes and their lips met.

David noticed the young woman that stood beside Rebecca. "Who are you?" The woman introduced herself to the group of frightened men. "My Name is Dina. Rebecca's car broke down in that bad snowstorm, so she and her friends stayed with me. We all became good friends and she called me here because she learned something."

David looked at Rebecca. "What did you learn Becky?"

She looked at him. She could feel it. *He isn't Jack. I am safe with him. But then there's Damian.* She looked over at Damian, who stood beside Jeremy. *He could be the Shadow Stalker. Well, I am going to find out. But not right now. I am too weak. I need to go home and come up with a plan to stop the Shadow Man once and for all.*

"David. Let's go back home. There's something that I want to tell you."

He helped her to her feet. The Shadow Man could see Rebecca from where he was standing. He was so close to her. *Soon. Very soon. You will be a piece of history again. Tanya will die the same way again and this time I will make sure that there is no way for her to come back - no way.*

CHAPTER 14

Rebecca was sure now that the man responsible for all her attacks was Jack - Jack Skye - Tanya's Jack. She clutched a pillow close to her heart. *It can't be though. Jack and I were meant to be forever and then I was killed. I never even got to see his handsome face again. After that horrible day. After that terrible night.*

Rebecca lay down in her queen-sized bed. She had left David's and come back to her own home. Victoria and Jared slept together in the guest room downstairs. They wanted a room on the lower level in order to make sure that Rebecca did not sleepwalk and hurt herself again. Fred slept in the room closest to Rebecca's.

Rebecca started to cry as the thought dawned on her that all her friends really cared about her and were going to stick by her no matter what happened.

"I can't believe this. It's the New Year and I don't feel like celebrating in anyway." She pulled the soft silky blanket over her body. She really missed all her friends, but especially Kristen. She almost started to cry again, but then she remembered that it was Jen's birthday. She hadn't heard from her best friend in years and now, suddenly, she wanted to call her. David had called her once in awhile over the years, but never Rebecca; not since her parents died.

She picked up the phone and started to dial Jen's number. The phone rang a while and then a familiar voice answered the phone. "Hello." Rebecca recognized Jen's voice. "Hey Jen. It's me, Rebecca!"

Tears began to form in Jen's eyes. She could not believe that Rebecca was calling her.

"Hi Rebecca! How are you? Wuz Up?"

Rebecca laughed, and then she started to cry. She really wanted to see Jen again. She really wanted to tell her everything, but she couldn't because she didn't want to involve her.

"I'm great. David and I are a couple now."

Jen couldn't believe the news. "It's about time. So when did this happen?" Rebecca thought happily about when it had happened and then she remembered and her face grew tense. "After Kristen's death."

Jen thought she heard Rebecca wrong. "What did you say? Kristen's death? I had no idea that she died. That's sad. I never liked her that much, but no one deserves to die."

Rebecca's face widened. "You said the exact same thing in one of my nightmares. Wow, I am so good."

Jen made a strange face. "Are you feeling all right? It doesn't matter right now. I have some news."

Rebecca paused. "What?" Jen announced that her boyfriend just got a job in Peacefulville. He would be moving there in the summertime and Jen would be moving with him. As for Malicine, she would be coming with her so she could attend Greenberry College. Rebecca was very excited, but then she became scared. *What if the Shadow Man was not stopped by then? He could go on another killing spree.*

"That's great Jen. I can't wait for you to come. By the way Jen, Happy Birthday! I have to go now. It's getting late. Bye."

Jen said goodbye and hung up the phone. Rebecca bit her lower lip. *Great, now what am I to do? It's January 1st, 1985. A New Year. I am supposed to be partying, or something. Not hiding out from a killer from my past life.* Rebecca got herself dressed.

"I am going to go to a club tonight. I'd better tell Fred to come with me. Just in case."

Rebecca got Fred and they went to pick up Dina and Jeremy.

Cathy decided she had enough partying for one day. She had been in a photo shoot that took most of the day, and she was very tired. Jeremy, of course, was a party animal and Dina was new in town.

Peter couldn't make it but he did say that he would try to come and meet them all again. Rebecca looked forward to meeting him again. *I wonder if any of my other friends are still alive?* Dina looked great. Her hair was curled and she wore a bodysuit and a nice pair of jeans.

Rebecca was wearing her silk dress, of course. Fred and Jeremy looked like twins, wearing almost the exact same jeans and tops. Finally the gang reached the Mixer and walked in.

The music was hip and there were a lot of teens dancing. Rebecca's eyes wandered until she spotted Damian sitting all alone with a beer in his hand. He looked drunk. *Perfect. This way I can get some information out of him.*

"Aah, guys, let's mingle." She had already told Fred of her suspicions, so he understood what she was up to as soon as he saw Damien. Rebecca walked up to him and he smiled.

She sat down next to him and he placed his hand on her shoulder and began to rub it. It made her uneasy, but she had to know the truth, so she went along with it. Dina walked around the club until she spotted a man cloaked in a black overcoat with his face covered. She realized that it must be the man who Rebecca said was stalking her.

So that's the Shadow Man, thought Dina, as she spotted Rebecca. She walked over to her and whispered in her ear. Rebecca followed her gaze and spotted the Shadow Man. She also noticed that Damien had disappeared.

It is Damian, then. Rebecca saw the Shadow Man, but he had not seen her yet. She told Dina to get Jeremy and Fred out of the club. Dina left to find the others while Rebecca walked up the stairs to where the Shadow Man was standing. She stood right behind him.

She could hardly believe it. She was about to finally unmask her past life murderer. "Damian." The Shadow Man swung around with a pipe clutched in his hand. The pipe swiped Rebecca's side and she fell over.

The Shadow Man was surprised to see her. He threw the pipe to the side, ready to finish her off for good. He grabbed her throat and started to choke her neck as hard as he could. She tried to get out of his grasp but he was too strong. She was loosing oxygen and her eyes began to close, but the she saw Damian running towards her carrying a chair. He smashed the Shadow Man in the head and Rebecca fell to the floor, coughing. *It's not him.* The Shadow Man took out his knife and slashed Damian's arm. Fred and Dina ran back into the club to see why everyone was running out of the club screaming and saw the Shadow Man.

Dina grabbed the fire extinguisher and ran up the stairs. Rebecca started to feel the familiar sensation in her body once again. She stood up and her hair began to flow. A strong wind suddenly blew through the club. Chairs and Tables began to fly everywhere. Dina froze.

The Shadow Man faced Rebecca, knowing what she was capable of with her powers. He took out his gun and shot three bullets at her. Rebecca stared at them with a great force.

The bullets suddenly stopped, suspended in mid air. The bullets then turned around and flew towards the door. Rebecca looked at the Shadow Man, and with a push of her mind, he went flying into the wall. She looked at Dina and Damian and with another push, she made them fly into the wall as well.

She could no longer control her thoughts or her emotions. The lights began to flicker and a fire started and surrounded her. The Shadow Man stood up and with strong strides, he walked up to her once again and grabbed her by the neck.

She struggled in his grasp, as the wind stopped and everything fell to the floor. The fire that surrounded her suddenly stopped. The Shadow Man pulled Rebecca up to his face and licked her cheek.

Rebecca's lips were then invaded by his sudden kiss. He then announced his ultimatum. "You may be strong now but you will not be able to use your powers on one day. That day is the day I will kill you…again. Happy New Year's, Tanya."

The Shadow Man threw Rebecca to the side and walked down the stairs and left the club. Rebecca got up and saw that Dina and Damian had been knocked out unconcious.

"I did this. I am so sorry." Fred and Jeremy came running back in and picked the two up and took them back to Rebecca's home. Rebecca sat by Damian, whose arm was still bleeding. She felt so bad for what she had done. She really needed to control herself. She still didn't know how to use her abilities very well.

Then thoughts of the Shadow Man came through her mind. *What did he mean by a day when I couldn't use my powers? I am really scared now. I wonder what day that is.* Damian awoke with a headache and Rebecca helped him sit up.

He looked at her, but she looked away, out of shame for what she had done. Damian touched Rebecca's face and she looked at him. Their eyes met and he drew her to him. Rebecca hesitated, but then their lips met. It was a sinful passion that swept over her.

The kiss didn't last very long, but it was still a kiss. Rebecca got up and then ran to her room, breathing irradicly. "What have I done?" Rebecca ran to her bed and began to cry. Damian sat on the couch, completely in love - with Rebecca.

Dina had finally awoke and was glad that Rebecca was alright. She wasn't mad at her, just shocked at what had happened. Still, she understood that trying to learn how to use such a power was harder than it looked.

Fred and Jeremy were proud of Rebecca. Her abilities were getting stronger. David got a telephone call from Jeremy and was told about the events that had taken place. He arrived at Rebecca's house an hour later.

He walked up into her bedroom and saw Rebecca, dressed just like Tanya. She was dancing in front of the large mirror. David started to cry. *I wish you would go back to normal, Rebecca.* He didn't bother her, he just walked back downstairs and told everyone that he would see them at school.

Jeremy looked at Fred. "I wonder what that was all about."

The next day Rebecca walked into her English class and everyone stared at her. She looked stunning. She sat in her seat and not a word came out of her mouth. Mr. Hiller walked into class and was surprised to see Rebecca dressed like she was from the olden days.

He taught the class a new lesson for English. Julie tried to talk to Rebecca but she ignored her. Julie could sense some tension between David and Rebecca. David gave Rebecca some glares. Not evil glares. Rebecca knew he was looking at her, but she didn't look at him. She kept her eyes on the homework that was written on the board.

Mr. Hiller announced to the class the news about the annual old class high school reunion. He asked everyone to attend to make the reunion a success. Rebecca had already bought a ticket for the event and was determined to go at all cost. The reunion was for the classes of 1940 to 1950, and she thought that the killer was bound to be there. But the reunion wasn't until March, and it was only January.

The lunch bell rung and the class was dismissed. Rebecca grabbed her purse and left as fast as she could. She didn't want to talk to anyone today. Jeremy and Cathy walked in the hallway together, hand in hand.

Jeremy told Cathy about the events that had taken place without her, and she was even more glad that she hadn't gone with them. She was frightened of the Shadow Man - very frightened. Julie was not as frightened though; she had already fought against him a couple of times. But even she knew that one day he would finish her for good, so she, too, was glad that she hadn't gone to the club with Rebecca and the rest of them.

Jonathan was glad that none of them had a serious problem with the Shadow Man. He didn't want anyone else to die. Jeremy kissed Cathy one last time before going to gym class and walked into the boys changing room. He took off his shirt and then his pants. He decided he needed a long hot shower to relax his nerves.

The water ran down his back. When he finished his shower, he put his shorts on, walked over to his locker and grabbed his shirt. Then he heard a noise. He stopped what he was doing and waited. He heard the sound again.

He put his shirt on and hurriedly made his way to the door, finding it locked. "Shit." A shadow of a person ran across the wall and he turned around. The shadow disappeared.

Jeremy saw that the back door was wide open and he could easily get out from there. He walked slowly through the hallway full if lockers and was almost at the back door when he suddenly tripped on a stream of marbles that were on the ground.

He fell to the ground, smashing his head on the hard floor. He struggled and got back up, but saw a hand holding a knife. The hand slashed at his face, and he fell over again. When he looked up, he saw the Shadow Man.

He became frightened and ran down to the front entrance. He pounded his fists against the door, sure that someone would hear his cries for help. He turned around to see where the Shadow Man was, but he was nowhere in sight. Then, a shadow began to creep up to him.

Jeremy decided to take a chance and ran to the back door, but the Shadow Man came into view. He stopped running and saw that a dead body was laying beside the Shadow Man. It was his good friend, Rick.

The Shadow Man walked up to him and, grabbing him by the face, drug him to the back corner of the locker room. He raised his knife and plunged it into Jeremy's chest over and over again. Jeremy fell over - he was dead.

The Shadow Man decided that he needed to do some real damage, so he took Jeremy's body and left the changing room.

Cathy had waited for almost two hours and still Jeremy had not come out from the gym. She started to get worried, but then she saw Rebecca, crying to herself. Cathy was mad at herself for being mean but she couldn't help it. Rebecca had been acting way out of line. She walked over to her and placed her hand on her shoulder.

Rebecca looked at her and then she started to cry even more. Cathy gave her a great big hug. "It will be okay. I am sure that the Shadow Man will get caught sooner or later." She stopped crying and Cathy asked her if she had seen Jeremy. She shook her head and both girls decided to go home.

At home Cathy and Rebecca found the whole gang waiting for them with tears in their eyes. Cathy noticed that Jeremy still wasn't there. *Oh no. It can't be Jeremy.* "What happened?" David took Cathy in his arms and explained to her how everyone had found Jeremy.

His body was found on the road outside of school. It looked like a hit and run but they weren't sure. Cathy began to cry, as did Rebecca. The next few days were spent making arrangements for the funeral.

Lana also came to the funeral. She had been released from the hospital and was feeling much better, although she was sad to find out about Jeremy. Dina didn't know Jeremy very well, but from the little time that she spent with him she knew he had been a good guy.

Rebecca ran straight to her room after the funeral. She took off Tanya's dress and threw it against the bed. She changed into her jeans and lace sweater. She went to visit Sofia and the barbershop and had her hair colored blond again.

She decided that she was not going to pursue this case anymore.

She was fed up. All she wanted was for all of the killings to stop. She came back downstairs to find everyone sitting in the living room. They were all surprised to see her dressed normally again.

Rebecca explained to them that she didn't want to be Tanya anymore. But David went up to her and shook her hard. "But you have to. If you don't you might be killed again and I love you too much to lose you. Do you understand me?" Rebecca looked at David. She really loved him; more than she had ever loved anyone in her life.

The rest of her friends came and gave her a hug, agreeing with David. Rebecca had to keep being Tanya until the Shadow Man was stopped for good. Everyone joined hands.

"For our lives and for Rebecca's freedom. Down with Shadow Man."

Rebecca looked a them all. She had to stop the Shadow Man, no mater what the cost; even if it meant her own death once more.

CHAPTER 15

The month of January passed by quickly. Cathy was still upset over Jeremy's death, but Rebecca knew that she would get through it somehow. Everyone decided to not let the Shadow Man take over their lives, and began to get back into their regular routine. Rebecca decided that she needed to think about things with David and Damian.

The tension was getting worse. The brothers seemed to argue even more than usual. Rebecca tried to mend things between the two, but it was hopeless. She finally decided to let them work out their differences on there own.

Rebecca and all the others were busy with the upcoming reunion. Everyone decided to preoccupy themselves by helping out, and Mr. Hiller was more than glad to have the help. He said he would give them all participation marks for helping out.

Lana was nicer to Rebecca than usual. Rebecca decided not to hold a grudge with any of her friends for being mean to her. She understood that they were all scared and didn't understand her. She loved to be Tanya, but she loved being herself more.

February was almost to an end and the reunion was just days away. Everyone was so excited. Cathy and Julie decided to go out to the mall to buy new dresses. Victoria was excited about the party as well. Mr. Peters invited her Aunt Madame Mystique.

Mr. Peters was familiar to Rebecca, as though they had met a long time ago. Rebecca thought that maybe he once had been Tanya's friend, but she really didn't know. She was happy that she would be going to her own school reunion for Harold High.

She knew that everyone would be shocked when she walked

into the party looking like Tanya, but she had a plan to capture the Shadow Man once and for all.

David and Damian finally put aside their differences, at least for a while, and went out to get tuxedos. Rebecca decided to let everyone stay with her in her house until after the reunion because she was scared. The Shadow Man's voice echoed through her mind once again.

"There is only one day you won't be able to use your powers. That is the day I will kill you."

Rebecca had a cold shiver run down her back. *I hope what he said is not going to happen.* David looked handsome in his tux. So did all the other guys. Dina and the other girls looked great in the dresses that they had bought.

Everyone had arrived except Rebecca. She had told everyone to go ahead. She had to dress herself up the exact same way as she once had dressed when she had gone to the prom. The prom. That was the day when she caught Jack dancing with another girl.

That was the day that she died. Tears flowed down her face. *But I'm back and I am not about to die again that easily. Not again.* Rebecca walked into the reunion. David saw her and his mouth dropped open.

Rebecca looked fantastic. Just like Tanya. Mr. Hiller saw her and was shocked at how beautiful she looked. Mr. Peters saw Rebecca and spit into his drink. "She looks like someone I used to know."

Peter was also at the reunion. Rebecca invited him. She wanted as many of her old friends there as possible. Rebecca walked over to Julie and the others. Julie and Cathy looked at Rebecca with amazement.

"Rebecca, you look great." Rebecca smiled and twirled around. Damian was staring at her in fascination. He had never seen such a beautiful woman as Rebecca in his whole entire life. All he wanted to do was to touch her, to love her. But he couldn't.

Madame Mystique arrived with Victoria and Jared. She was astounded at the sight of Rebecca. *Amazing*, thought Victoria and Jared. Jared extended his hand to Rebecca. "Would you like to dance Miss Arkenson, or is it Miss Bailey?" Rebecca giggled. "For tonight and all eternity it's Miss Bailey."

Jared and Rebecca started to dance. Victoria smiled at Damian. She didn't really like him because she saw Damian and Rebecca kiss. But she didn't say anything to anyone. She didn't want to cause trouble. Damian asked Victoria to dance and she accepted. Julie danced with Jonathan. Fred and Lana started to dance. Mr. Hiller asked Cathy if she'd like to dance. Cathy said alright.

David danced with Dina. Madame Mystique danced with Peter. Everyone danced the night away. Damian then asked Rebecca if he could talk with her. Rebecca hesitated but then gave in. Both snuck into the back room where they would both have some privacy.

Lana saw them leave, so she decided to follow them. David saw Damian with Rebecca as well and decided to see what was going on. Damian and Rebecca started to talk about that fateful night when both kissed.

"Rebecca, I love you. Why don't you consider being with a man who really loves you." Rebecca could not believe what Damian was trying to say. "I can't believe you. You know that I am in love with David. I will love him and only him, understand me."

Damian smiled a mischievous smile. From the corner of his eye he caught Lana watching them. He smiled. He then grabbed Rebecca from around her waist and then planted another kiss on her lips. The kiss was more passionate.

David was shocked. He had just got there, when he saw Damian and Rebecca kissing and he couldn't believe his eyes. *No wonder she was avoiding me*. He was mad. Lana was so shocked at what was going on that she didn't see a dark shadow sneak up beside her, until it was too late. She turned to see the Shadow Man.

He put his hand over her mouth, took out a needle and drove it through her head. She shook for a few moments and died. He hid her body and continued to watch Rebecca and Damian.

Damian noticed that Lana was gone, so he stopped kissing Rebecca. David couldn't stand it anymore so he left. Rebecca slapped Damian across his face and went back to the table.

Damian was satisfied, having done what he wanted to do. The Shadow Man left, knowing that there were a few more things he needed to take care of. David walked over to Cathy, not knowing what to do with himself, so he asked Cathy if she would dance with him. She accepted.

Rebecca came back to the table to see David and Cathy dancing together, but she didn't mind. She stood up, but a strange sensation ran through her body - a feeling of deja vu. Her mind began to alternate between Tanya's and her own.

She could hardly breath and when she looked up, she saw David and Cathy kissing. She felt like a piece of glass that had just been broken into a million pieces. She had never felt such anger and betrayal. The kiss lasted only a few moments, but then Cathy hugged David, squeezing him tightly.

Rebecca started to cry and grabbed her purse, feeling enough humiliation for one day. She ran out of the reunion and then she ran all the way back home. Jared saw Rebecca run out so he went after her.

He couldn't see her every well in the dark, so he called out to her, but she didn't turn around. He thought he had better go and tell the others, but a knife jabbed into his spinal cord. The Shadow Man raised him and dropped him.

Jared tried to get up but he could not. The Shadow Man grabbed him by the neck and heard the crack - Jared was dead. The Shadow Man disappeared.

Damian stood at the table, wondering what happened to Rebecca. He wanted to apologize for his behavior, but just then, Mr. Peters came up to him. "Hello there young man." Damian looked at Mr. Peters. "Hello Sir. Nice reunion eh?" Mr. Peters trembled a bit, but then responded. "Yes. Yes it is. I wanted to ask you a question about the girl who was with you and your friends."

Damian looked at him. *He must be talking about Rebecca.* The two sat down and started to discuss her. Madame Mystique looked all around but could not find Rebecca. Victoria also wondered what had happened to Jared.

***

The thunder crashed like a parade of beating drums in the silent night. Darkness covered the quiet streets of Peacefulville. A soft sobbing sound could be heard in the distance if you strained your ears. The sobbing was coming from an old Victorian house that looked like something from a painting.

The inside of the house was decorated with paintings and exquisite furniture, with a beautifully crafted, spellbinding staircase in front, leading to a large hallway full of mysterious bedrooms. Each bedroom held a sinister secret, but one held the most sinister secret of all.

Inside the room lay a young girl, on her queen size bed, writing in her diary. Lightning flashed throughout the girl's room, startling her, and she looked up. Rebecca's green eyes glistened as the lightning flashed through the room. Tears soaked her white silk dress.

She wiped her tears away and stood up. All the lights in the house were out, probably due to the nasty weather outside. She slowly walked towards her beautifully decorated glass window. Her parents had made the window for her, but now they were dead.

Rebecca could still remember them. She remembered how they had thrown a surprise party for her. It was such a great time of joy.

But she also remembered how the police had told her that her parents were dead.

"I am so sorry Miss Arkenson. Both of your parents died in the car accident. Sorry."

Rebecca started to cry at the memory. She clutched her locket. The locket that was given to her by her parents. Rebecca read the inscription to herself.

"To my darling daughter Tanya Annabella Arkenson. May you have all the happiness in the world. Always remember, we'll always be with you."

Rebecca began to cry like she had never cried before. But then something strange happened to her. It was as though a bolt of electricity went right through her body. A shiver ran down her spine. *Someone is coming. I can feel it. There is definitely someone in this house besides me. Oh don't be so ridiculous Rebecca. Honestly, my mind is so screwed up. What I need is to take a hot bath. That will sooth and relax me. Then all this stress will be taken away.*

"I better run a bath, then, if I am to relax. I guess I should change into something more comfortable. I'm starving. I should eat something. I better get some sleep too. I look like hell."

Rebecca got her bath ready and proceeded to her closet. She chose a comfortable nightgown to wear so she could have a good night's sleep. Rebecca picked out a Tweetybird nightgown that Julie had got for her. *Julie. I wonder what they all must be doing right now.*

***

"Attention all fellow classmates. The time has come to have our count down. Ready one…two…three."

Balloons fell from a net that was attached to the ceiling and everyone started to hoot and holler. David and the others sat at the table, clapping their hands, and Cathy started to laugh out loud.

Suddenly, a drop of blood fell on the table.

Cathy noticed it first. She looked up and saw Jared's dead body laying on the glass roof. The glass began to crack and the body fell through the glass, and landed on the table. Everyone screamed.

David was appalled by the sight, and Victoria started to cry as she ran to the dead body. Madame Mystique was surprised that she didn't sense the killing before it happened, but then she realized that Rebecca was missing. She glanced at the reunion banner and saw the date.

David saw the frightened expression on her face. "What's wrong now?" Madame Mystique pointed to the banner. "Today is March 2nd. It's the day Rebecca was killed - the day Tanya was murdered." David held his breath - Rebecca was missing.

No! No! He finally realized that she must have seen him and Cathy kiss and run home. *Shit.* Mr. Peters was shocked at the sight of the dead body, but Damian had already told him everything about Rebecca and her psychic abilities. He told Damian that Tanya also had those abilities.

Damian was shocked that Mr. Peters knew about Tanya. "Where's Rebecca know?" Mr. Peters asked. He had to ask the question twice before Damian also realized that it was March 2nd.

"Shit. Today is the day Tanya died. Rebecca is in trouble."

Mr. Peters stood up and walked over to the others. "What are you talking about? How do you know about Tanya's death?" David looked at the him and grabbed him by his coat. "What do you know about Tanya?"

Mr. Peters began to shake, but told him everything. He was Tanya's old friend, Daniel Peters. He had a sister named Samantha Peters. Finally, David let go of him.

"Okay. We have to find Rebecca before the Shadow Man finds her and kills her. We have to act fast because none of has any idea who the Shadow Man is."

Mr. Peters walked over to David. "Who killed Tanya before?" David looked at him. The poor man had no idea why everyone was freaking out. "Rebecca is Tanya. She was reincarnated. Some guy named Steven Lancaster killed her, but he's dead now. So now we don't know who has been stalking all of us."

Julie and the others huddled around David to hear what was going on, while Madame Mystique held Victoria, who was crying uncontrollably. Mr. Peters looked at all of the kids and a confused smile spread across his face. "Steven is not dead. He is very much alive."

Everyone looked at Mr., Peters in shock. If Steven was alive that meant Rebecca was in danger.

***

Rebecca lay her nightie on the bed and began to unlace her silk dress. Her slip was tight and she thought she was going to die from suffocation.

"This stupid slip. Why are these things so tight? Honestly. I do not find these things so womanly."

Before she could fully undress herself to change into her nightie the phone began to ring. Rebecca smiled uneasily and hurriedly laced her dress back up. Then she walked over to the phone and answered it.

"Hello!"

Rebecca waited for a response, but all she could hear was someone's constant breathing. "Hello! Is anyone there? Please tell me who you are?" Still, all that she could hear was breathing. She was frustrated and began to withdraw the phone from her ear. But then, suddenly, the person began to speak.

"Don't put the phone down Tanya, or else."

Rebecca shuddered. *It can't be. This can't be happening again.*

The voice now sounded so familiar to her, like a voice from her long forgotten past. *Something is going to happen. Stop it. Put the phone down.*

"Look you sicko. I think you dialed the wrong number. This is not a 900 number. So get bent!"

The voice on the other end became angry. "Don't you dare put the phone down, bitch! Not unless you really want to die...again."

Rebecca froze; such anger, such fury. *It can't be!* Rebecca was paralyzed with fear. The phone was still in her hand, so she slowly put the receiver close to her mouth and began to speak. "Why are you doing this to me?" There was a slight pause but then the person began to speak. "I am coming for you, my love, and this time I'll make sure you never come back again."

Rebecca cried out. She dropped the phone and began to pace back and forth. Her eyes darted from the door to the window. *What should I do?*

"I better lock all the windows and secure all the doors."

Rebecca ran downstairs and locked the front door. The large deadbolts were sure to lock anyone, or anything, out. There were similar bolts on all the windows, and she made sure that she checked the whole entire house three times before she was satisfied and went back to her room.

Her diary remained open on her bed. She walked over to the telephone and picked it up, but there was no dial tone - it was dead. Suddenly, there was a loud bang. She turned around to face her window; nothing. She went over to her window and locked it. Even though her bedroom was on the third floor, she didn't want to take any chances with a possible entry for thieves, robbers, and other such creeps.

She lit a few candles and shadows began to dance on her bedroom walls in many shapes and sizes. She was fascinated with the shadows. After her parents died, the shadows were the only things that made her feel safe, but these shadows seemed different from the usual ones. With her back to the front door, she took in a deep breath. She thought that if she calmed herself a little, she would feel much better.

Who could be doing all of this? Why me? I thought this was all over with when I died the first time and now it's starting all over again. I will never be free until I find out all the secrets of my past. Only then will I finally be free. Rebecca shook her head, but suddenly froze when, from the corner of her eye, she saw the shadow of an intruder.

Rebecca gulped, and with all the strength she had left, she turned around. Her long blond hair flew like an angel in fury. There before her stood the man from her past; the man who had been stalking her; the man who called himself, the Shadow Man.

He looked at her and began to snicker evilly. Rebecca yelled at him. "What are you doing here? Why don't you leave me alone?"

The man stopped laughing. "Do not be so silly Tanya, or should I say Rebecca. I told you that I would be coming for you, and look; here I am. But this time you wont be coming back; ever."

The Shadow Man took off his jacket and his hood, revealing to Rebecca what she dreaded - the true identity of the Shadow Man. She started to cry out and the Shadow Man laughed.

"Surprised, Rebecca?"

CHAPTER 16

Mr. Peters explained to Rebecca's friends that Steven Lancaster was still alive. "He is still alive. I guarantee it."

Victoria blinked and then looked at Cathy and Julie. Cathy shook a little, but then she had to ask. "Then who is he?" Mr. Peters had his eyes to the floor. He fidgeted with his fingers. "Steven Lancaster did have an accident. His parents had a bad divorce and Steven was forced to live with his mother. His last name was changed to his mother's maiden name - Hiller."

Cathy's eyes widened, and Julie fell in the chair. "That means that Mr. Hiller is Steven. Oh my God. I saw him leave the reunion a while ago."

They looked at each other in horror. All at once everyone shouted. "Rebecca!" Everyone ran out of the reunion, knowing that they had to save her at any cost. David sat in his car and started the engine.

"Hang in there Becky. I'm coming."

***

Rebecca's face was wide with horror. There in front of her stood her teacher, Mr. Hiller. "Mr. Hiller. How could you?" Mr. Hiller laughed. "Call me Steven. I missed you so much Tanya."

Rebecca tried to run out of the room, but Steven grabbed her and threw her against the wall. "Still trying to play that same game, aren't you." She couldn't believe it. Her teacher was Steven Lancaster. She tried to speak but could not. She then tried to focus her mind on a weapon, but nothing would happen.

Steven saw Rebecca staring at the chair. He started to laugh. "I told you that you would not be able to use your powers against me. You couldn't use them when I killed you before."

She stopped looking at the chair and looked at him. *What? That means I had these gifts when I used to be Tanya.* Steven reached towards her and forced himself upon her. Their lips met in an intense kiss. His tongue made its way into her mouth and she bit his lip, causing it to bleed.

Steven let go of her and touched his lip. He saw blood on his fingers and gave Rebecca an evil glare. "Why, you bitch. We could have lived happily together but you were in love with Jack. I took care of him as well."

Rebecca looked at him and her eyes filled with tears. *He killed my Jack. My Jack!* Steven continued on. "You didn't like me because I was younger than you." Rebecca looked at Steven. *Younger, I thought he was in his twenties when he killed me.*

"You liar. You were in your twenties." Steven looked at Rebecca. "Stupid girl. I was only seventeen. I was rich, I could have been any age. I liked the age of twenty."

Rebecca then remembered the article she had read in Wendy's scrapbook. "But I read an article that you died." He started to laugh. "Oh that. I was a reporter working for the newspaper, so it was very easy for me to fake my own death. My mother and father had a divorce and my last name was changed to my mother's last name, Hiller."

Rebecca was shocked at how she had been deceived. *He was only seventeen.* She could not believe it. She suddenly felt trapped and did not know what to do. She only hoped that David and the others would realize that she was missing. *Please. Help me.*

***

Madame Mystique began to hear Rebecca's plea for help. "Rebecca's in trouble. Steven is there with her." David started to speed his car up even faster. *I won't let her die…not again.*

***

Steven looked at Rebecca. "I still love you."

She turned to face him and spit in his face. "But I don't love you. I could never love you. I will never love you. You are a repulsive man. I cannot believe that I ever became friends with you."

Steven gripped Rebecca's shoulders and moved his face close to hers. "Remember what happened to you the last time you rejected my love? You died."

Rebecca tried to get out of his grasp but he was too strong. His face grew tense and anger engulfed him. He raised his fists at her. "I didn't want to do this, but I refuse to have you love anyone else. Die Tanya."

Steven walked menacingly towards her. Before she could even scream, his strong hands came forward. The hands then gave her a push into the direction of the window with an immense force, slamming her into the window. Pieces of glass scattered on to the floor. She looked up at him.

"You think you can kill me, but I am not the same girl Steven. I am much smarter than you think." Rebecca grabbed Steven's hand and pulled him with all of her strength. They both went crashing through the window and the locket that was around Rebecca's neck slipped off and fell to the floor. Glass stabbed at their bodies.

Both of their screams echoed throughout the silent streets of Peacefulville as they descended to the ground. Rebecca was swept into a memory of when she fell before, and she could remember crying for help. The memory faded and she was confused. *Why is this happening to me again?* Both now landed against the cold wet ground. Her neck twisted but did not break. She heard something crack in her ankle.

Steven's head smashed against a rock. Rebecca lay on the wet ground as rain soaked her once beautiful white silk dress. Now the dress was swirled with different shades of red from her blood, as well as Steven's. Her eyes shut and she collapsed, as did Steven. Both lay on the ground, unconscious.

CHAPTER 17

The sirens of police cars echoed throughout the quiet town. Rebecca could hear an ambulance. David parked his car and then everyone got out. Cathy spotted Rebecca lying on the ground, surrounded by broken glass and her dress covered with blood.

Everyone ran to her and David held her in his arms, crying. Everyone else then began to cry as well. They all thought that Rebecca was dead, but then she opened her eyes. She saw David's tears come down his handsome face.

Madame Mystique noticed a black shoe on the ground nearby. She picked it up and studied it. There was fresh blood on it. She looked up towards the window that Rebecca had been thrown out of. *I wonder what happened.*

It was Jonathan who finally noticed that Rebecca was alive. "Hey, she's alive." David looked down at her and saw that her eyes were open. He cried out with relief. Julie and Victoria ran over to Rebecca and gave her a hug and she suddenly remembered what had happened.

She moved David away from her and tried to stand up but she could not. Her ankle began to bleed heavily. *I must have broken it when I fell.* Rebecca scanned the ground for Steven but he was nowhere to be seen. Steven was gone; he got away.

Rebecca gave everyone a frightened look and began to speak in a scratchy voice, but instead, she only spit out blood. She looked up at everyone and they all seemed worried. She then tried to talk again.

"Mr. Hiller is Steven. He tried to kill me…again. But I took care of him."

Madame Mystique raised her eyebrow at what Rebecca had said before, went over to her, and asked her what happened. She told everyone what had taken place; about the phone call, how Steven had tried to force himself on her and how she had grabbed him and they both crashed through the window; but now he was gone.

The police searched the grounds, but did not find him. Rebecca knew that he would come back to get her. She was rushed to the hospital, where she found out that her ankle was very badly broken. This was doubled by the fact that she had already sprained the ankle once before.

The doctor gave her a shot to calm her and help the pain go away. Her face was also cut badly, and the doctor told her that her scars might be permanent, but he would try to fix them.

David did not leave her side. He didn't want to abandon his love. Cathy and the rest waited outside. The nurse finally announced that visiting hours were over, but David did not want to leave. The nurse pointed out that there were two police guards standing by Rebecca's door and they were going to make sure that no one got in without going through them first.

David kissed Rebecca one last time and left her room. Madame Mystique was worried about her because she had told her that she could not use her powers. She thought that was strange, since Rebecca's powers were not magical, they were part of her mind.

Rebecca slept peacefully in her room, although it was very depressing, with its white walls and musty smell of medicine. She twisted and turned in her bed, remembering things from her past.

David and the others decided to go back to Rebecca's house and gather their belongings, preferring to stay at the hospital until she was better. David also wanted to take a look around to see if he could find Steven. He thought that he might still be in the house.

When they arrived, there were still a few police cars around. Cathy shivered and looked at Victoria and Julie. She suddenly real-

210

ized that both Dina and Lana were missing.

***

Dina sat patiently on the first floor of the hospital. She had decided to stay at the hospital instead of getting her stuff. She didn't really need to get anything, she was fine the way she was. Dina's tired eyes began to shut and, before she knew it, she was a sleep.

A disfigured man, with a badly cut face, watched the hospital from outside. His hand was also cut, with several pieces of broken glass stuck in it. The pain was very great but nothing surpassed how angry he felt. His eyes were full of hatred. He was going to kill Rebecca even if it meant he had to die himself.

The figure pulled out a knife. It was the same knife that killed Jack, and Steven smiled at the memory. He remembered how he had killed Jack, only two days after he had murdered Tanya. *Now that was fun. I enjoyed killing him.*

As the blade shimmered in the moonlight, he remembered that this was also the knife that he had killed Isabella with, when she found out that Steven had planned to kill Tanya and Jack. So, before Isabella went to the police he had killed her. During that time Steven was working for the local newspaper, and her death had made a great story for his paper.

When he killed her, he dumped her body into some well in Crescent Point. Steven smirked at the memory of his handy work, but then frowned. "That stupid girl. She thought she could escape her own death by dragging me out of the window with her. She was wrong. Dead wrong."

His face hurt, but he put on his Shadow Man uniform and walked towards the hospital. *Time to end things like they were supposed to have ended. I am going to kill Tanya so she does not remember any other secrets of her past.*

Rebecca heard her name being called. Her eyes opened and she sat up in her bed. There was no one in the room with her. She put her hands on her face. "I am going to go bonkers in this room." She got out of her bed and tried to walk to the door, but she couldn't.

The nurse walked into the room and found her sprawled across the floor. "Hey, are you okay?" She helped her back to bed and told her to stay still. *Great, I am stuck here.* Rebecca turned her head to see a shadow cast against the changing screen.

She began to scream and the nurse came running back in with the two guards. Then, as suddenly as it had appeared, the shadow was gone. The guards told Rebecca to relax and the nurse went to get some hot water so she could wash her face.

When she left the room, Rebecca was alone again. She knew that her eyes were not deceiving her; she had seen a shadow. She cried for help in her mind, hoping that someone would hear her. Madame Mystique heard her loud and clear.

***

Madame told everyone that Rebecca was in danger, and they raced out of the house and to the hospital.

***

The lights in Rebecca's room turned off, and she couldn't see a thing until her eyes finally adjusted to the dark. Even then, all she could see was the door's frame and light coming from the window.

She got out of her bed, afraid that Steven was in her bedroom once again. The door opened and he walked in, carrying a binder with him. Rebecca couldn't see his face until, suddenly, the lights turned on. She screamed.

Steven raised his hand and slapped her across the face. She fell on the bed and looked at him. He pulled out his blood covered knife. Rebecca screamed for the guards but no one came to her aid.

"It's no use. They are dead. I took care of them all. Just like I am about to care of you Rebecca... Tanya." She threw the pillow at him and limped to the door as fast as she could, but Steven tripped her.

He kicked her hard in her stomach and she could hardly breath from the pain. The nurse walked into the room carrying a bowl full of boiling hot water and saw Rebecca sprawled against the floor. Then she saw Steven.

"Oh my God."

She then threw the boiling hot water on Steven's face, and he yelled in agony. His eyes were shut, but he still managed to take his knife and stab the nurse with it.

"Run, Rebecca!"

She pleaded with Rebecca who was scared stiff, but managed to get up and limp out of her room. She called for help but there was no one on her floor. All the nurses had already left for the night and the late shift had not arrived yet.

Rebecca limped until she finally reached the elevator. She got in and, scared and confused, pressed every button. The elevator started to close, but she caught a glimpse of Steven running towards her. Thankfully, the door shut before he reached her.

The elevator started to go down but then it stopped and began to go back up. She started to panic. "No. No." The elevator stopped and opened. Rebecca was on the last floor of the hospital, which was abandoned. She had first been to this floor when she was a volunteer there, and had to know everything about the hospital.

She pressed the buttons to go down, but the elevator was stuck, and wouldn't budge. She had no other choice, so she got out and slowly limped down the dark hallway to the staircase. She opened the door and began to go down, but she saw Steven walking up the stairs, so she retreated.

Rebecca finally got to the final level of the staircase, which led to the roof of the hospital. She had no where else to go, so she ran out onto the roof and hid behind a wall. She didn't hear Steven coming up the stairs, she was so delusional.

***

Dina woke up when she heard screaming, and when she stood up she realized that there were many police cars outside of the hospital. She ran to the front doors but they were shut. Dina banged against them, but they wouldn't open. She realized that Steven must be after Rebecca.

She ran to the elevators and pressed the buttons. It seemed to be taking forever, but then she noticed that it was jammed on the highest level. She ran to the staircase and ran all the way upstairs to Rebecca's room, but she was gone.

"Oh no."

Dina turned around to find her, but a pipe hit her in the head and she fell to the floor. She was taken to Rebecca's bed, and Steven took some water, threw it all over her and grabbed an electrical wire. She woke up to see him holding the wire. She rolled off the bed just as he was about to strike her.

She grabbed the pipe and hit him across the face with it, rammed him in the back and ran out of the room. *Rebecca must be on the last floor of the building.* She ran to the stairwell.

Rebecca drifted off to sleep and her eyes fluttered open. She began to walk around the roof in another sleepwalking trance. She walked towards the ledge, back to the door and then back to the ledge again. Dina could not find her on the last floor so she decided to check the roof. When she got there, she saw Rebecca walking around.

Dina ran towards her, Steven stood in the way. "Going somewhere?" Steven held his knife. Dina knew she had to wake Rebecca up. She ran to the other side of the roof in an effort to sidetrack Steven, but he walked another way and he finally caught Dina.

Rebecca started to sleepwalk into Dina's direction, so she ran over to her and began to shake her. "Rebecca. Wake up!" She moaned, but Dina stopped shaking her. She felt the blade drive deep into her back.

Steven then pulled out the knife as Rebecca started to walk into the direction of the ledge. Dina, who was struggling to stay standing, ran and pushed her away from the ledge. Steven then grabbed Dina and threw her against the wall. Rebecca fell and hit her head, and suddenly awoke.

She had no idea what was going on, but the sound of police trucks and cars made her stand up and walk towards the ledge. She couldn't see very well, but she could see David and the others standing outside of the hospital. She shouted to them but they could not hear her.

Jonathan looked up and saw her, so he shouted to everyone. The police shined their light at her, temporarily blinding her. She opened her eyes and saw the others waving their hands as if they were warning her of something.

"What? I don't know what you guys are saying?"

David swore underneath his breath. They were trying to tell her to turn around. Steven was standing behind her. David ran to the entrance of the hospital and broke down the glass door. Damian stood with Cathy in his arms, who was scared out of her mind for her friend. Victoria was hugging her aunt. Rebecca saw Julie pointing, so she finally gave up and turned around just as Steven slashed the knife at her. She screamed and slipped.

Rebecca fell over the ledge but managed to grab a hold of it. Steven stood in front of her, knife in hand. She screamed when she looked down, noticing that the drop was very high. Steven began to step on Rebecca's hands.

"No, please don't. Leave me alone."

Rebecca screamed as loud as she could. Her hands kept slipping but she still grabbed onto the hospital's ledge with all her might, not wanting to let go for anything. She had made it this far without getting killed, and she was determined not to let it end like this. Rebecca looked up to see Steven glaring down at her from the ledge, clutching his trustworthy knife. He bent down and then started to slash the knife at her hands. She kept dodging the blade, but even she knew that she could not do that forever.

Steven's twisted face glared evilly at her. "After I kill you I will then kill myself. That way you and I will be together forever and that way I will make sure you can never escape me and get reborn again."

Rebecca had to do something quick, or else, so she gave her intuition another try. *Please work.* She concentrated her mind on anything loose on the hospital roof that she could use to protect herself with. Her mind focussed on a garbage can that was in the corner. It started to hover above the ground, and she opened her eyes and saw Steven pull out his longest knife. He could easily reach her with this one.

Steven looked at Rebecca. "Any last prayers, Tanya? Oh, ok then…die!"

She screamed and then pushed the can with her mind. It quickly hovered towards Steven and slammed into him, hard enough to cause him to fall over the ledge. However, he managed to grab a hold of Rebecca's feet and she shrieked and began to struggle. She looked down at him, and saw that in his hand, he still had a hold of his knife.

Julie saw Steven dangling off the building. "Oh my God!" Cathy started to cry out on horror. Damian just stared out in a daze. *This can't be happening.* Victoria screamed.

Rebecca struggled. "No, let go of me!" Steven was holding her feet as they both dangled of the ledge. She screamed as Steven penetrated the knife into her leg and she felt the warmth of fresh, hot blood pour down her cold limb. *Please, someone help me!* David ran up the stairs as fast as he could. "Don't worry Becky. I'm coming."

She tried to kick Steven, but he had a strong hold of her feet.

"I am going to kill you again, Tanya. I told you I was going to. Whether you like it or not. Jack didn't want to die. Neither did Isabella; but they are both gone."

Rebecca then concentrated her mind on Steven's hand with the knife in it, and he swore at the sudden, unbearable heat of it. His hand was burned and he was forced to let go of her with it, giving her the ability to move one of her feet. Her leg pained along with her ankle. Anger and pain consumed her. Rebecca gathered all the strength that she had left in her free foot and slammed it into Steven's face.

The impact forced his other hand free and he looked up at Rebecca one last time before his body dropped to the ground far below. Rebecca turned her head so that she could see him fall and land on the electrical fence that was in front of Julie and the others.

His body wretched as he began to sizzle. Rebecca was so appalled at the sight that she suddenly lost her own grip. She began to scream but before she fell, a strong hand grabbed a hold of hers. She looked up to see that the hand belonged to David. He pulled her back on the roof.

Cathy and the others were relieved that she was all right. Rebecca looked back down to where Steven's lifeless body lay and saw his blank eyes stare up at her as he whispered his last words.

"Tanya, I love you. I'll come back for you again…"

Rebecca turned her eyes away from the horrid sight. She heard a noise and turned to see Dina. David ran over to her, relieved that she wasn't dead. She would be alright. Rebecca was happy that the nightmare was finally over. Steven was dead.

EPILOGUE

The secrets from Rebecca's long forgotten past were finally resolved, and she could move on in her life. David and Rebecca decided that they were going to also move on with their lives. David asked Rebecca to marry him, and she accepted with glee. However, they decided to wait until school was finished to get married.

Rebecca and the others were devastated when a few days after Steven died, the dead bodies of Lana, Keith and a few others were discovered. A memorial service was held for all of the poor souls who were murdered by Steven, the Shadow Man. Rebecca prayed in the church for everyone to have peace. She hoped that all of the people who died were safe and happy in heaven.

The summer finally arrived. Julie moved in with Jonathan, and Cathy started dating Damian. Victoria found a job that would preoccupy her. Fred moved into Rebecca's big house, and Cathy and the others also decided that it would be fun to live with Rebecca in her house. Jen was also on her way.

Nighttime had arrived and Peacefulville was actually peaceful. A bony hand, covered in blood, rose out from the ground. It pressed against the official welcoming sign which read, "Welcome to Peacefulville," and smeared its blood all over the sign.

Headlights shown down the road, and the hand went back into the ground. A young girl and a young man slowed down beside the sign. The man rolled down his girlfriend's window and said, "Hey, the map says that this is the place, but the town's name changed."

The young girl looked at the name with a surprised expression on her face. The sign now read, "Welcome to Bloodsville."

The young woman looked to her boyfriend who started to laugh. "Oh well. Here we are, Jen. Home sweet home."

Jen looked at the sign once more - Bloodsville. *Rebecca never told me that the town's name had changed. Oh well.* Jen's boyfriend started up the car, then drove into town. As the car left, she thought she caught a glimpse of a man standing in the shadows near the welcome sign. *No way.* Jen looked back and saw nothing. *I guess I must be homesick already.*

The young couple finally reached Rebecca's home. They got out of the car and together they said, "Welcome to Bloodsville!"

SECRETS OF MY PAST PART TWO VENGEANCE WITH A TWIST

He came back with out a warning…

He came back to finish what he had started two years ago…

He came back into their lives without them even knowing that he was back…

This time he is not leaving until he gets his revenge on the girl who beat him at his own game; the one who dared to challenge him; the one who defeated him. He is the Shadow Man and this time he is looking for vengeance - vengeance with a twist.

Rebecca thought it was all over, but she was wrong. It is far from over because some secrets of the past are never revealed, and when they are not, those secrets will come out from the past and haunt you in your present. This time Rebecca will find out the hard way that some secrets never die, and even if they do, they always manage to find a way to come back.

This time Rebecca will face the ultimate challenge, but will she be able to win this time, or will evil finally get its vengeance?

To find out, read the second chilling novel of the Secrets of My Past Trilogy and this time, get ready for the scare of your life.

ABOUT THE AUTHOR

H.D. Myst is a 19-year-old who was born and raised in Toronto, Ontario. Humdip has always wanted to publish a book and now he has done that. He promises more spine tingling novels that will scare the living daylights out of all of his readers. *Secrets of My Past Book One: Shadows of My Past* is his first full length novel and he hopes that the readers will enjoy it and be excited for the release of Book Two of the trilogy. He enjoyed writing this book, although he even scared himself while writing it.